MORAINE VALLEY COMMUNITY COLLEGE LRC/LIBRARY
PALOS HILLS, ILLINOIS 60465

MORAINE VALLEY COMMUNITY COLLEGE

3 5029 00281990 0

Y0-CCF-635

[WITHDRAWN

HQ 784 .T4 H615 2002
Hoffman, Eric, 1950-
Changing channels

DEMCO

(WITHDRAWN)

Changing Channels

by Eric Hoffman

Redleaf Press
St. Paul

©2002 Redleaf Press
All rights reserved.
Cover photograph by Dane Penland.
Illustrations by Christine Tripp.

"Turn It Off, Change the Channel, Leave the Room!" ©1996/1997 2 Spoons Music.
    Used by permission.
"Dad Threw the TV out the Window" ©1988 Bill Harley. Used by permission.
"50 Things That I Can Do instead of Watch TV" ©1996/1997 2 Spoons Music.
    Used by permission.
"Buy Me This and Buy Me That" ©1996/1997 2 Spoons Music. Used by permission.
"The TV Way" ©1996 Bill Harley. Used by permission.
"Count to Ten and Try Again" ©1996/1997 2 Spoons Music. Used by permission.
"Use a Word" ©1986 Red and Kathy Grammer. Used by permission.
"Talk to Me" ©1996/1997 2 Spoons Music. Used by permission.
"Sharing" ©1996/1997 2 Spoons Music. Used by permission.
"A Ballet Dancing Truck Driver" ©1996/1997 2 Spoons Music. Used by permission.
"That's What I Like about You" ©1996/1997 2 Spoons Music. Used by permission.
"The Power in Me" ©1996 Cathy Fink and Ken Whitely. Used by permission.

Published by: Redleaf Press
                    a division of Resources for Child Caring
                    450 N. Syndicate, Suite 5
                    St. Paul, MN 55104

Visit us online at www.redleafpress.org

ISBN 1-929610-22-X

CONTENTS

Part Three: Supporting Children's Self-Esteem

INTRODUCTION

Welcome to *Changing Channels,* a collaborative effort between Redleaf Press and musicians Cathy Fink and Marcy Marxer. This is the second in a series of three books to accompany Cathy and Marcy's CDs. The others are *Help Yourself* (2001) and *Nobody Else Like Me* (forthcoming, 2003). This book was written to help you use the music on this CD to help children and families in your program think critically about what they see on TV, resolve conflicts productively, and develop healthy self-esteem.

Cathy and Marcy's music is a great tool for creating curriculum on a variety of topics, and this book will show you how. So open the pages, and turn up the sound!

How to Use This Book

This book is divided into three sections. The first focuses on media awareness; the second on conflict resolution; and the third on building self-esteem. Each section begins with a short introduction to the subject as it affects young children. This is followed by the songs and activities. You'll find sheet music and complete lyrics for each song, followed by a brief introduction to its developmental content. You can use the sheet music to play the song on a guitar or a piano; many of the songs also work well for singing in circle times without instrumental accompaniment. Or simply sing along with the recording, using the lyrics sheet. We suggest that teachers listen to the whole CD several times and become familiar with the songs before introducing them to children.

Activities help you explore the topic of each song with children ages three to eight. The first activity for each song gives ideas for using the song itself with children during circle time. The rest of the activities show you how to expand upon the song throughout the day. The final activity for each song helps you involve parents in the discussion too!

The age range for each activity is noted at the top of the page. The activities are designed for a wide age range of children; be sure to evaluate them with your own group in mind, and adapt as necessary to make them work for the children's developmental level.

As more and more children with special needs are included in child care centers and other early childhood programs, it's essential to adapt curriculum to their needs. Many of the activities in this book contain adaptations for children with disabilities (see the Variations).

Changing Channels (Cambridge, Massachusetts: Rounder Records, 1998) is available as a CD or as a cassette from Redleaf Press, 800-423-8309.

Taking Charge of the Media

What do you do when you visit a friend or relative for a few days? If you want to be invited back, you help with some chores, fit in with family routines, bring a small gift, and give a compliment or two. Who wants a houseguest who is crude, never listens, and encourages conflict?

Yet every day, the homes of many of the families we work with are filled with terrible houseguests. These guests get invited in because they make people laugh and forget their worries. They get in because families have to get dinner on the table, and parents have no one else to be with their children while the work gets done. They get in because adults hope children will learn something worthwhile from them.

They get in when families turn on the TV without taking charge of the guest list.

Research shows that TV, movies, and videos can help children learn nonviolent, thoughtful, creative ways to engage the world. But that same research shows that much of so-called children's programming makes them more aggressive and less imaginative. It also shows that the advertisers who pay for programs are becoming better and better at encouraging children to pester parents into buying their products. How? In part, advertisers are doing more studies on how to sell to children. In addition, the deregulation of children's TV allows companies to create programs that are really half-hour commercials for toys.

Even if we completely shield children from the media, they often pick up these influences from their peers, in our classrooms, and in their neighborhoods. So what can teachers do?

Help families take charge. Since most of children's media exposure takes place at home or with their family, you won't be effective in changing children's viewing habits without the families behind you. Take the time to discuss your ideas with parents and find out what they will support. You will probably discover that many parents are worried about what their children are learning from TV and movies, but they feel powerless to change the situation. The information, songs, and activities in this section can help you and your families take an active role in choosing the kind of programming they allow into children's lives. "Turn it Off, Change the Channel, Leave the Room!" can help children stay in touch with their feelings when confronted with images they don't like. "The TV Way" explores the difference between media fantasies and real life. "50 Things That I Can Do instead of Watch TV" and "Dad Threw the TV out the Window" look at alternatives to being a couch potato. "Buy Me This and Buy Me That" was written to counteract the commercialism children confront on the screen and in the stores.

Here are some additional resources that can help schools and families take charge of the media:

Cantor, Joanne. *Mommy I'm Scared.* San Diego: Harcourt Brace, 1998.

Giroux, Henry A. *Stealing Innocence.* New York: St. Martin's Press, 2001.

Levin, Diane E. *Remote Control Childhood.* Washington, DC: National Association for the Education of Young Children, 1998.

Levine, Madeline. *See No Evil.* San Francisco: Jossey-Bass, 1998.

Ready at Five Partnership. *Channeling Young Children Away from Media Violence.* Baltimore: Author, 1996. (Available from Redleaf Press.)

Walsh, David Allen. *Dr. Dave's Cyberhood.* New York: Simon and Schuster, 2001.

American Academy of Pediatrics Media Matters Campaign at www.aap.org/advocacy/mediamatters.htm

Center for A New American Dream at www.newdream.org

Center for Media Literacy at www.medialit.org

Children Now at www.childrennow.org

Educators for Social Responsibility at www.esrnational.org

KidsFirst! at www.cqcm.org/kidsfirst

LimiTV at www.limitv.org

National Institute of Media and the Family at www.mediafamily.org

Turn it Off, Change the Channel, Leave the Room!

TV programs and movies can teach children lots of facts, but what they do best is to bring up feelings, especially in young children. This is fine when the intent is to help children understand their feelings and empathize with the characters they are seeing. But many shows use feelings to mesmerize, rather than inform. Their goal is to monopolize children's attention.

We have all seen children staring at the screen, wide-eyed and barely moving. We've probably all been in that state ourselves! As early childhood educators, we know that young children don't normally stay that way for long. After a few minutes, they need to move and to play out and talk about their experiences. But that takes their attention away from the show.

So how do programmers keep children's eyes on the screen? Since young children can't keep track of a story line for long, children's shows often focus on stimulating the senses and emotions. Watch a children's action segment or commercial. You will see new scenes flash across the screen every few seconds, with drastic changes in perspective, distance, and color. This visual collage is usually tied together by a soundtrack with a driving beat. There is time for feelings to emerge—most often excitement, fear, or craving—but no time to think about what they've seen. Before children have a chance to ask, "What was that about?" the image has changed.

Without our support, many children are unable to say "Enough!" And since adults care so much about the plot, families often discourage children from turning off the TV or walking out of a movie. "Turn it Off, Change the Channel, Leave the Room!" can help children understand that it's okay to slow things down, pay attention to their feelings, talk about what they've seen, and move away if their bodies are telling them to do so.

Be sure to inform parents about activities you are planning that encourage children to turn off their TV or walk out of movies. This can create tremendous family conflict if parents don't support your efforts.

Use these children's books to explore the feelings that come up when watching the media:

Brown, Marc. *Arthur's TV Trouble.* Boston: Little, Brown and Company, 1995.

Gilmore, Rachna. *Ellen's Terrible TV Troubles.* Markham, Ontario, Canada: Fitzhenny and Whiteside Ltd., 2000.

Novak, Matt. *Mouse TV.* New York: Orchard, 1998.

Turn it Off, Change the Channel, Leave the Room!

By Marcy Marxer
©1996/1997 2 Spoons Music, ASCAP

Turn It Off, Change the Channel, Leave the Room!

by Marcy Marxer

(©1996/1997 2 Spoons Music, ASCAP)

If you sit down on the couch to watch TV
And there's something you don't really want to see,
If it makes you feel alarm
Then it loses all its charm,
You are stronger, you're in charge of what you see.

chorus:
Turn it off, change the channel, leave the room,
You can go and find some other thing to do.
If you don't like what you see, get away from the TV
Turn it off, change the channel, leave the room.

If the golf announcer's talking to his shoe
Or a tiger's eating up a kangaroo,
If they're fighting and they're hissing
Or they're holding hands and kissing,
Yuck, I'll go find something else to do!

chorus

You can wrinkle up your nose and make a face
You can say, "This is a cultural disgrace!
This TV show is a bore
I'm not watching anymore,
I think I'll put a new show in its place!"

chorus

Ages: 3–6

THE OFF BUTTON

When young children see something on TV that scares or confuses them, they may not know they can speak out and turn off the TV. The Off Button game gives children a way to talk about their past experiences and practice taking action.

Materials

Changing Channels CD
CD player
a piece of paper with a large red Off Button on it

Directions

1. Attach the Off Button poster to the wall.
2. Invite a group of three to six children to play the Off Button game.
3. Listen to the song "Turn it Off, Change the Channel, Leave the Room!"
4. Ask the children to remember what happened in the song. What did the singers see on TV? How did they feel about it? What did they do? Play the song again if the children can't remember.
5. Ask the children to talk about scenes on TV or in movies that they remember and didn't like.
6. After a child finishes describing a scene, ask if she would like to hit the Off Button for that scene. If she says "Yes," have her run up and push the button.

Discussion

These questions will help the children participate in this activity:

- What kinds of shows do you like to watch? How do they make you feel? What kind of shows don't you like? How do they make you feel?
- When something scares or confuses you, how does your body feel?
- What can you do if you don't like a TV show? A video? A movie?
- What can you do if you don't want to watch a show but someone else in your family does?

Variations

1. For children with limited mobility, use a portable gong or a buzzer that you can bring to the child instead of the Off Button poster.

2. Give each child a card with Off written on one side and On written on the other. As children describe shows, take a vote on who would watch it and who would not. This may bring out gender differences in show preferences, so be prepared with discussion questions: Why do you think mostly girls like this show? What is it about this show that appeals to girls? Could a boy watch this show if he wanted to? If a boy is being teased about a show he likes, how can you help him?

SAFETY CHECK

We will be most successful at helping children keep themselves safe when they are watching TV if we also show them how to keep themselves safe at other times, particularly in their play. The Safety Check game provides ongoing opportunities to teach children what to look for. It's easiest to start with physical safety issues. Once children understand how it works, they will be able to think about emotional safety as well—even when they are watching TV.

Materials

Directions

1. At various times and places during the day, call for a Safety Check. For example, do a check when the children are building with large blocks or other construction toys, during a cooking project, when a teacher is setting up a climbing activity, or when the children are playing a chase game. Start with small groups when you are introducing the concept.

2. Ask the children to help you inspect the activity to make sure it is safe.

3. Talk with the children about what you are looking for and what you find. For example, if the children are building with large blocks, you could say, "I'm looking for blocks that might fall over and hurt someone on their head or on their toes. Does this corner of your spaceship look safe to you? How can we make it safe?" Don't focus only on parts you feel are unsafe. Point out places that look safe, as well, and state why they look safe to you: "I see this wall of your house is very straight and strong. It looks safe to me, does it look safe to you?" You can also use the Safety Check to reinforce safety rules: "Our rule is that blocks can only be built up to your shoulders. Does your building follow that safety rule?"

4. Work with the children's ideas until the activity seems safe to you. Ask, "Does this pass the Safety Check?" Be sure to offer your congratulations!

5. Try to have several Safety Checks each day, in different areas of your classroom.

6. When the children understand the Safety Check process, they will often start to do their own—a good time to expand the concept to cover the children's conflicts, as well. Ask, "How can we help everyone feel safe before we solve this problem?"

Discussion

These questions will help the children explore the issue of safety:

- How can you tell when something is unsafe? How can you tell when it is safe? What do you look for?
- How do you feel when you are in a situation that is unsafe?
- What are some ways you can tell another person that they are not being safe with you?

Variations

1. Make official-looking signs that say "Inspected for Safety." Post them when an activity has passed the Safety Check.
2. Make Safety Inspector hats, badges, or medals for the children to wear while they participate.
3. Give your Safety Inspectors flashlights.
4. Once the children understand how to conduct a Safety Check of the physical environment, extend the concept to emotional safety. In a conflict, or when the children seem disturbed by a media scene, tell them you are going to do a Safety Check on people's feelings. Ask them if they feel okay about what is happening or what they are seeing. Figure out how to change it if they say no.

Ages: 3–8

THE MAGIC BUTTON

We want our children to be able to push the Off Button during shows that they don't like. Magic Buttons help children learn about the opposite, equally important side—knowing that they can say "Yes" to their imaginations when their fantasies and wishes are not harmful.

Materials

wood and cardboard scraps
buttons
other small, glittery objects
glue (older children can use glue guns, when supervised)
paper and pen
glitter glue or pens (optional)

Directions

1. Ask the children to create a Magic Button with the art materials, one that they can pretend will make wishes come true.

2. Ask the children what will happen when they press their Magic Button. What will they wish for?

3. Write down their responses. You might want to display the wishes on the wall for everyone to see. Use them in documentation of the children's learning or as conversation starters on subsequent days.

Discussion

Here are some questions that will help make this activity fun:

- Is your button an On Button that makes something happen or an Off Button that makes something stop?

- What would you wish for yourself? What would you wish for a friend? For someone in your family? For someone in the community you think could use your help?

- If your class is talking about someone from history (for example, Martin Luther King Jr.), what do you think that person would wish for? What would you wish for them?

- Will Magic Buttons work if you make a wish that might hurt another person? How can you turn your Magic Button off?

Variations

1. Make a Magic Button Book or a Magic Button Poem by combining the children's responses.

2. Magic Buttons can be incorporated into a variety of activities. The children can include Magic Buttons in their drawings and paintings. Hang Magic Buttons outdoors and the children will use them to talk about their fantasy play. Hang a Magic Button Target, such as a pie plate, and the children can throw bean bags or soft balls at it. Then tell a Magic Button Story when they hit it. Draw Magic Buttons on some of your blocks, and the children will build them into their structures.

3. Include some of your Magic Button Stories in a Wishes and Dreams Time Capsule (see page 150).

INVOLVING FAMILIES: THE MEDIA REPORT BOARD

Children need the support of their families if they are going to learn to be discriminating media viewers. The Media Report Board shows children that families can work together to decide what is safe for them to watch.

Materials

paper and pens
tacks or other ways of posting reviews

Directions

1. Set up an area of a bulletin board that is accessible to all families for reading and writing. Label three sections: TV Shows, Videos, and Movies. In each section, post a page with four columns: Name of Show, My Child's Reactions, My Opinions, and My Name. Have pens readily available.

2. Point out the display to the families. Encourage staff and families to add media reviews to the lists. You may need to write the first reviews to get the process started.

Discussion

Keep these points in mind when setting up this activity:

- Encourage the families to put up a balance of positive and negative reviews.
- Some families may not want to participate if they are embarrassed about their TV watching. They may be willing to add comments to existing reviews rather than write new ones.
- By listening during the children's play or during group discussions, you may be able to tell which shows the children are watching. Approach the parents with this information, and ask for their opinions on the shows. Ask them to write their opinions on the Media Report Board, or offer to take their dictation.

Variations

1. Some families may want to add a section on computer games.

2. Post reviews from local papers with a sign saying, "Do you agree?"

3. Put out two kinds of stickers for the families to add to their reviews, one for highly recommended shows and one for shows to avoid.

4. Add a section to the board for recommendations on alternatives to TV—local activities, homemade materials, family games, and so forth.

5. If you have families members with limited vision, you might consider tape-recording reviews for them to listen to. Ask them to tape-record their own reviews for your transcription later.

DAD THREW THE TV OUT THE WINDOW/50 THINGS THAT I CAN DO INSTEAD OF WATCH TV

"I'm bored!" Turning the TV on is an easy way to solve this problem, but it's not the only way. Some children reach for crayons, or a ball, or a book. Some families play games or music together. Many families, however, are stuck in TV mode. They may need help creating new routines.

Many parents want to set limits on the number and the type of programs their children watch. Setting these limits is an important place to start, but limits work best when there are positive alternatives that are easily available. If parents want to say "No" to TV, then they have to give their children something to say "Yes" to! And if the alternatives are fun and not presented as punishment, then they may find that creativity, learning, and physical activity can be habit-forming for children—and for themselves as well.

Teachers can help parents with the following:

- decide what limits to set and how much they are willing to compromise
- brainstorm alternative ways to keep the children occupied, especially when the adults are busy
- model the behavior they expect from their children, including limiting their own screen time
- use their best listening skills when the children are upset by the changes
- remember that some families need to change slowly, while others can just throw the TV out the window

Use these books to help the children learn about alternatives to watching TV:

Miller, Sara. *Better than TV.* New York: Bantam Doubleday Dell, 1999.

Ziefert, Harriet. *When the TV Broke.* New York: Viking Kestrel, 1989.

Gordon, Lynn. *52 Alternatives to TV.* San Francisco: Chronicle Books, 1996.

Heilbroner, Joan. *Tom the TV Cat.* New York: Random House, 1989.

Dad Threw the TV out the Window

By Bill Harley
©1988

Dad Threw the TV out the Window

by Bill Harley

(©1988 Bill Harley)

It was in the morning, a sunny Saturday,
We turned on the TV and on the couch we lay.
We watched our favorite program and another couple shows
When our dad came in the room, folded arms and tapping toes.
He said: "Kids, turn off the TV now there's lots of things to do,
Your beds aren't made, the chores aren't done, the sun is shining too."
I said, "Oh, Dad, I'm busy now, I've gotta watch this show."
I guess we should have listened, but how were we to know?
'Cause then he walked across the room and then he pulled the plug,
He lifted up the television and skipped across the rug,

He opened up the window, and then we
   screamed, "Dad! No!!"
But he gave the thing a heave and we
   watched the TV go.

chorus:
Dad threw the TV out the window, the
   window
I think he's finally cracked,
Dad threw the TV out the window,
We got a feeling that it isn't coming back.

When I saw it go, when I heard it crash
I knew that things at our house would
   soon be changing fast.
Our dad looked out the window and he
   mumbled, "My, oh my!"
My brother looked out too and said, "I'm
   gonna die!"
And that night after dinner when we
   went to watch the set
All we found was nothing I said, "How
   could I forget?"
My brother lay down on the floor and
   moaned, "What will I do?"
I said, "Why don't you move away?"
He said, "The same to you!"
But then he told a joke and I told two or
   three
And the one about the elephants made
   Dad fall on his knees
And Mom did her impression of a duck
   that couldn't fly
That would have made you wet your
   pants and maybe even cry
All because —

chorus

Life without a television wasn't what I
   feared

I didn't really miss it though some
   friends thought I was weird
I didn't miss commercials and all
   the blood and guts
And all the stupid shows my brother watched that drove me nuts
But then one sunny Saturday our
   dad could not be found
We looked high and low when from
   his room we heard a sound
We ran into his room to see what it
   could be
And found our father hiding there,
   watching a TV
I said, "Oh Dad, now really, you
   ought to be ashamed!"
He said kind of sheepishly, "I want
   to watch the game."
We picked up the TV and waltzed
   across the room
And gave the thing a heave and
   waited for the boom

chorus:
Oh, we threw the TV out the window, the window
Guess we've finally cracked,
We threw the TV out the window,
   we got a feeling that it isn't coming back.

Ooooooh, we threw the TV out the
   window, the window
Guess we've finally cracked,
We threw the TV out the window,
   and we'll live if it never comes
   back.
Yes, we'll live if it never comes back!

50 Things That I Can Do
instead of Watch TV
by Cathy Fink
(©1996/1997 2 Spoons Music, ASCAP)

My brother watches TV shows that make
  me scared and spooky
My sister watches boring shows that I just
  think are kooky
And sometimes there's just nothing on,
  and once the TV broke!
There's 50 things that I can do
I bet you'll think of 50 too
There's 50 things that I can do instead of
  watch TV

Draw a picture, read a book
Open up my eyes and look
At pretty flowers, birds, and squirrels
Go outside and turn and twirl
Bounce a ball or play catch
You haven't caught up with me yet
Play with blocks, play with cars
Play with dolls or look at stars
Play a game of make-believe
Where I'm a giant ice-cream machine

There's 50 things that I can do
I bet you'll think of 50 too
There's 50 things that I can do instead of
  watch TV

Go exploring in my yard
Make my mother's birthday card
Sing a song or make one up
Drink milk from my favorite cup
Make a puppet with my hand
Play air guitar in a rock and roll band
Play with my toes, wiggle my nose
Sit and watch my garden grow
Swing on a tree, say my ABCs
Tell me what you think of me

There's 50 things that I can do
I bet you'll think of 50 too

There's 50 things that I can do
  instead of watch TV

Close my eyes and count to ten
Cluck like a chicken and walk like
  a hen
Call my grandma on the phone
Watch my doggy chase a bone
Feed the fish, make a wish
Put some cereal in my dish
Catch some bugs and watch
  them eat
Look what I can do with my feet
Hop on one foot, hop on the other
Shake a rattle for my baby brother
Make an airplane out of clay
Dance the jig or do ballet

There's 50 things that I can do
I bet you'll think of 50 too
There's 50 things that I can do
  instead of watch TV

Bounce a ball over my head
Make a fort over my bed
I can have a gooey time
Mixing up my own green slime
Call my friends from down the
  street
Have our own Olympics meet
Imagine things that you can do
When you pick what you want
  to do

There's 50 things that I can do
I bet you'll think of 50 too
There's 50 things that I can do
  instead of watch TV

Ages: 6–8

DRAMATIC PLAY

The song, "Dad Threw the TV out the Window," tells the tale (based on a true story!) of a father who found a dramatic way to break his family's TV habit and how his children helped him do the same. Older children will enjoy creating a play based on the song, and people of all ages will enjoy watching it.

Materials

Changing Channels CD
CD player
copies of the words to the song "Dad Threw the TV out the Window"
a cardboard box, about the size of a TV set

Directions

1. Invite a group of six to eight children to create a play about TV.

2. Listen to the song "Dad Threw the TV out the Window."

3. Hand out copies of the song lyrics. Ask the children who want to participate to help you act out the song.

4. Choose one child to be the father and one the mother. The rest can be the children.

5. Go over the song one section at a time. Have the children invent movements for the lyrics. When they have practiced a section, try acting it out with the music.

6. Have the children make props for the play. In particular, ask the children to decorate the box to make it look more like a TV. The children may want to create other props as well, such as costumes and a pretend window.

7. It may be enough for younger children to create the play and "perform" it for friends at the end of the day. Older children may want to rehearse the play over time and schedule a performance for parents, or for other groups of children in the school or program.

Discussion

Help the children decide how to act out the song by asking, "How would you feel, and what would your face look like, if . . .":

- someone threw your TV out the window?
- you went to watch TV, but it was gone?
- you caught someone doing something that the person had told others not to do?
- you were caught doing something you had told others not to do?

In order to stimulate further discussion, ask the children questions like these:

- Why do you think the dad in the song got so frustrated that he threw the TV out the window?
- Does anyone in your house ever get fed up with the TV? What happens then?

Variations

1. Most children will want to do the motions while the song is playing, but some groups may want to learn the words and sing the song while they put on the play. Assign one child to be the sound-effects person. Use a cymbal or other way to make a CRASH!

2. Have the children put on the play for groups of children or for families.

3. If your group likes dramatics, they will probably like Activity Charades as well.

Ages: 3–8

WHAT TO DO COLLAGE

Can't think of anything to do besides watch TV? A collage of alternative activities can be a great visual reminder that there are plenty of other fun ways to spend your time.

Materials

Changing Channels CD
CD player
magazines
scissors
white glue or clear tape
large paper or cardboard pieces

Directions

1. Invite a group of up to six children to listen to the song "50 Things That I Can Do instead of Watch TV."

2. Ask the children to find magazine pictures of the activities mentioned in the song or other activities they could do instead of watch TV.

3. Have the children cut out the pictures and glue or tape them onto paper or cardboard.

4. If someone can't remember any of the activities mentioned in the song, have the group create a list everyone can use. Play the song again if the children can't remember, then keep adding to your list.

Discussion

Here are some questions that can help the children focus on the project:

- What activities do you like to do by yourself? Which ones can you do with friends?
- Which activities are loud or active? Which ones are quiet?
- Which activities can you do at home if your parent needs to get some work done? Which activities can you do at school if you want to spend some quiet time alone?
- Which activities require that you buy things? Which can be done for free?

Variations

1. The children can draw pictures or take photos of activities for their collage, instead of using magazine pictures.

2. Make a group Favorite Things to Do Collage with each child, adding one picture of their favorite activity.

3. For groups that include children with visual impairments, make a "recording collage." Children can take turns speaking or singing into a tape recorder about their favorite activity.

THE INVENTION KIT

Here's something to dump on a table on a rainy day, or even a sunny day. Why turn on the TV when you can bring out . . . the Invention Kit. Watch out, though—adults will have as much fun as the children do.

Materials

file box or other sturdy container
plastic drop cloth
various parts of old machines and toys (be sure they are clean and safe)
small boxes, plastic trays, scraps of plywood, heavy cardboard, or other materials for bases
buttons, jar lids, smooth stones, sticks, acorns—anything small that can be glued
string and ribbon
masking tape
white glue (school-age children can use glue guns, with supervision)
scissors
markers

Directions

1. Cover a table or floor area with the drop cloth.
2. Spread out the contents of the Invention Kit in the center.
3. Set up four or more work stations along the edge of the space. Place glue, scissors, markers, and tape at each station.
4. Have each child pick out a base.
5. Let them glue, tie, and tape together any "invention" they want. Affix the invention to the base.
6. Be sure to have a drying area set aside—inventions can take up to a day to dry.

Discussion

While working on their inventions, some children may enjoy discussing these topics:

- What is an invention? Who makes them? Can children invent things?
- Look around the room. Can you find something that was invented? What does it do? What do you suppose people did before it was invented?
- What is your favorite invention, at home and at school?

Variations

1. Make up a "patent certificate" for each invention. Children can write or dictate about their invention's name, use, and why it is unique. Use these descriptions to create a book of inventions, with illustrations or photos.

2. Groups of children can create a large invention together out of appliance boxes, carpet tubes, branches, wood, tires, rope, and lots of duct tape.

3. Invite a real inventor into your classroom.

4. Let older children use real tools, with supervision, to take apart broken, unfixable machines—record players, typewriters, toasters. Avoid items that hold electrical charges, such as TVs and VCRs— these are marked with a small lightning symbol. An adult may need to loosen screws and bolts for preschoolers. This activity requires close adult supervision if the machines have power cords, to make sure they don't get plugged in.

5. Give your inventions away at the Swap Meet (see page 44).

ACTIVITY CHARADES

Older children are very good at charades and other guessing games. This one is based on the activities mentioned in the song "50 Things That I Can Do instead of Watch TV," but it can easily be expanded to include the children's own ideas.

Materials

Changing Channels CD
CD player

Directions

1. Listen to the song "50 Things That I Can Do instead of Watch TV" with a group of four or more children.
2. Ask a child to pick an activity mentioned in the song without saying it out loud.
3. Have the child act out their activity, without words, while the rest of the group tries to guess what it is.

Discussion

To stimulate discussion after the charades, try asking:

- What are some times when people have to communicate without words?
- What are the ways people communicate with each other without using words?

Variations

1. Invite someone who knows American Sign Language to teach children the names of their favorite activities.
2. If you have children who are physically unable to participate in charades, create a set of picture cards of tools or other objects people might use as part of a favorite activity. Have the children pick a card and show it to the group, then ask the group to try to guess the activity that goes with it.

3. Ask the children to find objects that they would use as part of their favorite activity. Have them put it in their own box or bag. Divide the children into pairs. Have one child close their eyes, feel inside the other child's bag, and guess what the object is and for what activity it is used.

Involving Families: Book Reports

Reading is always an excellent alternative to watching TV. You can encourage families to read to their children by letting them take home any duplicate books you have in your school library. This fun "family homework" assignment also gives adults a way to get involved in their child's education.

Materials

a variety of children's books that you are willing to send home with children
markers, crayons, or colored pencils
white drawing or copier paper
envelopes, large enough to hold a book and art supplies
a box or crate to hold the books
a small table or other space for the above materials
bulletin board or other display space

Directions

1. Place a set of markers or other art materials and a small stack of paper in each envelope. These will be your borrowing envelopes.

2. Create your lending library by placing the crate of books and the envelopes on a small table near your parent entrance. You may want to include a checkout system for materials as well—a clipboard to sign or a set of cards in a file box.

3. Send a letter home for each family describing the Book Report activity (see sample letter). Post a copy near the table.

4. Add Book Reports to your display space as families bring them in.

5. If possible, take a picture of the family or child holding the book and place it next to their report, so that children can easily identify the books. As an alternative, make a color copy of the book cover or use the dust jackets of hardcover books.

Discussion

Here are some questions that can help you introduce the children to the idea of Book Reports. The families can use these ideas to help their children get started:

- Which were your favorite parts of the book? Who were your favorite characters? Did you like the illustrations?
- How did the book make you feel?
- If you were writing this book, which parts would you change? Would you end the story the same way or would you change the ending?
- Does everyone have to share the same opinion about a book?

Variations

1. You can introduce the Book Report concept at group time by reading a book and discussing what people think of it; then let the children draw pictures or dictate their ideas about the book.

2. Invite a local author to talk to your class about their book.

3. For children who are unable to write or draw, have a tape recorder that the family can borrow to record their Book Report.

Dear Families,

Are you looking for something you can do with your child at home besides watch TV? Now you can borrow children's books from school! We have set up a lending library near the front door. Feel free to take a book home to read with your child. Then, we would love it if you would help your child create a Book Report. Here's how:

1. Help your child select and sign out a book. Please take only one at a time.

2. If you want to borrow some art supplies to make your Book Report, a set of markers in an envelope can be signed out.

3. Read the book at home with your child. Young children often like to hear the same book many times!

4. Ask your child to help you make a Book Report for school. Some children will want to draw a picture, while others will want you to write down their words.

5. If your child can't think of what to say or draw, ask questions, such as:

    - What happened in this book?
    - Which was your favorite part?
    - Who was your favorite character?
    - How did you feel at the end of the book?
    - If you were telling this story, is there anything you would do differently?

6. When you bring in your report, one of the teachers will take your picture with the book for our Book Report display.

7. Return the book and art supplies within three days so other families can borrow them. If the book has been damaged, ask the teacher for supplies so you can help your child repair it.

8. Borrow another book. Borrow books as many times as you like! Perhaps someone else in your family would like to do a Book Report for us.

We also invite you to come into the classroom and read to the children, then help them write Book Reports in school. When you read to the children, listen to them and write down their words. You are helping them on the road to reading.

Thanks for being your child's best teacher—

BUY ME THIS AND BUY ME THAT

Branding used to be what ranchers did to their cattle. Today, it's what advertisers want to do to our children. Soft drinks, shoes, fast-food chains, toys, breakfast cereals—manufacturers want children to ask for their product and to feel cheated if they don't get it. Advertisers have become very sophisticated at creating brand loyalty in children, even in toddlers, using animation, trick photography, music, tie-ins at restaurants, and TV shows that are commercials for toys. They know how to include all the needs and desires of childhood—friendship, happiness, self-esteem, security, power—and how to make children believe that they can't feel fulfillment without their product.

Research shows that young children can't pick out what is real in a commercial. They don't know where the commercial ends and the TV show begins. They don't even understand a commercial's purpose! In a toy or grocery store, they will decide what they want based on the excitement they felt watching the commercial or by looking at the packaging. And since many toys are designed to be purchased with accessories, children demand more to be satisfied with their play.

Children can't resist the branding strategies they encounter without adult guidance. We can gradually teach them to watch commercials with a critical eye. We can create an advertising-free zone in our classrooms by eliminating commercial logos and cartoon characters from the materials we buy.

And we can use songs such as "Buy Me This and Buy Me That" to get a conversation going with the children about commercialism.

These children's books touch on issues of commercialism and possessiveness:

Brumbeau, Jeff. *The Quiltmaker's Gift*. New York: Scholastic, 2001.

Stanley, Diane. *Rumplestiltskin's Daughter*. New York: William Morrow, 1997.

Tusa, Tricia. *Maebelle's Suitcase*. New York: Aladdin, 1991.

Williams, Vera. *A Chair for My Mother*. New York: Greenwillow, 1983.

Buy Me This and Buy Me That

Oh, we're go-ing to the grocer-y store To get some food for sup-per,
I get to ride in a wheel-ie cart and be my dad-dy's help-er. And
as I'm rid-ing up and down, Hey, look at the toys__ that I have found.
Dad, will you buy me that shin-y red truck? Can I have that doll, can I
have that duck? When you push a but-ton this dog says, "Ruff" Can you
buy me all that stuff? It's buy me this__ and buy me that,__
Buy me that__ and buy me this,__ He smiled at me and blew a kiss,__
Do you think mon-ey grows on trees? If so we'll have to plant some seeds. You
can't have eve-ry-thing you want And don't for-get to say "Please!"

By Cathy Fink & Marcy Marxer
©1996/1997 2 Spoons Music, ASCAP

Buy Me This and Buy Me That

by Cathy Fink & Marcy Marxer
(©1996/1997 2 Spoons Music, ASCAP)

Oh, we're going to the grocery store
To get some food for supper,
I get to ride in a wheelie cart
and be my daddy's helper.
And as I'm riding up and down,
Hey, look at the toys that I have found
"Dad, will you buy me that shiny red
     truck?
Can I have that doll, can I have that
     duck?
When you push a button this dog
     says, 'Ruff' "
Can you buy me all that stuff?"

It's "Buy me this and buy me that,
Buy me that and buy me this,"
He smiled at me and blew a kiss,
"Do you think money grows on trees?
If so we'll have to plant some seeds
You can't have everything you want
And don't forget to say, 'Please!' "

Oh, I'm watching TV with my mom
We do it every Saturday
With our pj's on we snuggle up
And watch cartoons and laugh away
Then a kid comes on with a power laser
And a special magic orange phaser
"Oh, Mom, can I have a brand new toy?
You know I've been a real good boy
I want that toy from the TV show
It'll make me happy, I just know
I'll be awesome when I play
Mom, can I have it today?"

It's "Buy me this and buy me that,
Buy me that and buy me this,"
She smiled at me and blew a kiss,
"Do you think money grows on trees?
If so we'll have to plant some seeds
You can't have everything you want
And don't forget to say, 'Please!' "

Oh, we're going to the beach today
Just me, my mom and dad
We'll build a sand castle ten feet
     high
It's the most fun that we have
Then Dad says, "Look, there's a
     shiny bike
With a bugle horn and a go-fast
     stripe!"
"Oh, honey, if you buy that bike
     today
Then I want fancy new rollerblades
Knee pads, wristguards, cool
     looking shades."
I almost couldn't believe my ears
And this is what I said

It's "Buy me this and buy me that,
Buy me that and buy me this,"
I smiled at them and blew a kiss,
"Do you think money grows on
     trees?
If so we'll have to plant some seeds
You can't have everything you want
And don't forget to say, 'Please!' "

THE GROCERY STORE

Shopping at the grocery store is a common experience for young children. Some preschoolers think of it as a place where people can buy whatever they want, endlessly. Others realize that some families can buy a lot more at the grocery store than others. The Grocery Store game will help early elementary children see that most people have to make choices when they shop.

Materials

Changing Channels CD
CD player
clean, empty boxes and containers from food or other grocery store items (Try to use containers from basic foods, such as eggs and milk, rather than heavily advertised items such as sugary cereals.)
red, yellow, and blue paper
clear tape
paper bags
envelopes
play cash registers or other containers to hold play money

Directions

1. Cut out circles, triangles, and squares from the colored paper. Make each shape about one- to one-and-a-half-inches wide.

2. Tape colored shapes, from one to three, on each empty box. Larger or more popular items should have more shapes.

3. Place three of each colored shape in envelopes, one envelope for each child in the group. These shapes are the children's play money.

4. Set up a play grocery store on tables and shelves, using the empty food boxes.

5. Listen to the song "Buy Me This and Buy Me That" with your group.

6. The song starts with a trip to the grocery store. Ask the children if they remember what happened in this part of the song. If they can't, play the first verse and chorus again.

7. Ask the children to describe any similar experiences they have had at the grocery store.

8. Explain that you have set up a grocery store and that you will give them some "money" to buy items from the store. To buy an item, they have to match the colors and shapes on the package to the money in their envelope; then give the money to the cashier. They won't have enough money to buy everything they might want, so they will have to decide what they can get with the money they have.

9. Ask for volunteers to be cashiers who will check "prices" and help bag groceries.

10. Give each child an envelope of play money.

11. Open the store.

12. The children can construct houses and kitchens in other parts of the classroom to play with the grocery items.

13. Have the children restock the store when the play is done.

Discussion

To help children think about food and grocery stores, ask them:

- How do you decide what you want to buy? Do you look for food that will help you grow? Do you look for bright packages? Do you look for foods you've seen on TV?
- Where does the food that you buy in a store come from? How does it get to the store?
- How do people get money to pay for groceries?
- How do people get food when they have no money?

Variations

1. You can also use colored-dot stickers on index cards for the money system; place stickers directly onto the boxes for prices.

2. Set up a system for the children to earn more money.

3. For children with visual impairments, use three different textures, such as sandpaper, felt, and nylon. Glue material onto paper or cardboard and cut into shapes for money; glue material directly onto the boxes for prices.

4. Preschool children enjoy grocery shopping, too, although most can't understand a complex money system. Try a simplified version with one color and one shape for money.

DIGGING FOR TREASURE

Can you ever have enough? Not if you believe commercials—there is always something else to buy. But we don't have to make children feel that everything is scarce to counteract commercialism. It's fun to have plenty using natural or recycled materials and when everybody has enough.

Materials

natural treasures, such as rocks, shells, acorns, wood shapes, and pinecones

recycled treasures, such as old marker tops, juice can lids, and buttons

sandbox, dirt area, or sensory table filled with sand or dirt to bury the treasure

hose, plastic pipes, pieces of lumber, rope, or safety cones to define the treasure digging area, if necessary

small plastic shovels for younger children, larger metal shovels for older children

bags, buckets, boxes, or other containers to hold the treasure

Directions

1. Gather the treasures. The children can help you find them on a nature walk or can bring in juice can lids from home.

2. Bury the treasure. Again, this can be done with the children's help. For younger children, bury most of the treasure in the first 9 inches of sand or dirt, or hide it inside a layer of hay. For older children, you can bury treasure up to 18 inches down. You don't have to hide it too carefully or make the search too difficult—just fill up the area with treasure. Set aside some of the treasure, in case you need to add more.

3. Give the children shovels and a treasure container. If you are working in a small area, you may have to limit the number of children who can dig at one time.

4. Dig for treasure. Some children prefer to dig with their hands. Make sure the children using metal shovels aren't too close to smaller children.

5. If treasure is getting hard to find, add more. Make sure there is plenty for everyone, so that the children don't feel as if they have to fight over it.

6. Set up an activity where the children can share the treasures, such as:
   - a group gluing project, on a piece of cardboard or a large Treasure Box
   - an outdoor kitchen, where the children can cook the treasures and mix them with sand and dirt
   - a garden decorating project, where the children can set their treasures into the garden beds around the plants

Discussion

Here are some fun questions to ask about treasure and treasure hunting:

- What makes something a treasure?
- Can people or friendships be treasures?
- Do you have something at home that is your treasure?
- Why would someone hide treasure?
- What are some ways to share treasures?

Variations

1. Spray painting treasure in silver and gold is always a big hit!

2. For children who are unable to dig, you can hide treasure in a sensory table or plastic swimming pool full of hay, cloth scraps, or leaves.

3. With older children, spread colored aquarium rocks in a sand table and use sifters to separate the rocks.

4. Draw a map showing a path to the treasure, or use clues to the treasure's location.

5. Set up a Treasures of Nature table. Bring back items from a nature walk to add to the table.

Junk

Commercials don't always lie, but they rarely tell the whole truth. Young children aren't ready to analyze advertising, but they know when they've gotten a toy or other product that doesn't live up to its hype.

Materials

a product you have purchased that didn't do what was promised on the packaging or in an advertisement

letter to the families asking for the children to bring in similar toys or other products (see sample below)

Directions

1. Show the item you brought in at group time. Describe your experience with it: how and why you bought it, any advertising you saw for it, why it didn't work the way you expected, and how you felt about it.

2. Ask the children if they have ever bought toys that didn't work the way they expected. Ask them to bring in the toys if possible, so everyone can see why they didn't work.

3. Send a letter to the families asking them to participate.

4. As the children bring in toys, have them show the items to the group and describe their experiences and feelings.

Discussion

Here are some questions to ask the children about the toys they bring in:

- What did you see in commercials or in the packaging of this toy that made you want to buy it?
- Were you happy with it when you got it? Why or why not?
- If it didn't meet your expectations, how do you feel about it?
- What would you like to say to the people who made this toy? What changes would you suggest to them?
- How do the people who make commercials try to sell you products?
- Is everything that you see or hear on a commercial true?

Variations

1. Write down the children's stories. Create a display that includes the stories and some of the toys and packaging.
2. Write letters with the children to the companies that made the toys. Post any responses as part of your display.

Dear Families,

Does your child have any of these?

- A toy that broke too easily
- A toy that was too difficult to use
- A toy that just wasn't as much fun as its commercials promised

We have been talking about TV commercials at school, about how they try to convince us to buy things and how they sometimes promise more than they deliver. We are looking for examples of toys that you have purchased for your child that didn't work the way you expected.

Please have your child bring in his or her "junk" toy. If you have the packaging, send that too. We'll use it to help the children watch TV and make purchases with care.

Thanks for being your child's best teacher—

INVOLVING FAMILIES: THE SWAP MEET

Commercials are designed to make children want more and more stuff that costs more and more money, with little regard for the work that goes into earning that money. The Swap Meet will help children think about what they can do to get the things that they want and see that giving stuff away can be as much fun as getting it.

Materials

children's art and carpentry projects
table and tablecloth
pens and paper for signs

Directions

1. Ask the children to create projects, or to choose ones they have made in the past, that they would like to give away. See the Invention Kit (see page 26) for one way to create interesting projects.

2. Set the projects out on the table where the families and students can see them.

3. Create a list of small jobs that people can do around your classroom, school, or community. Post it by the Swap Meet table.

4. Post a sign that describes the Swap Meet rule: You can take one item from the table for every job you complete.

5. Ask the families to add small items that they would like to give away.

6. Put up a Swap Board where the families can list larger items they want to give away. Include a corresponding list of bigger jobs that can be done for these items.

Discussion

To bring out some of the issues behind the Swap Meet, ask the children:

- What are the ways people obtain the things that they want or need? What are the ways people get rid of things they no longer want or need?

- Is there something you want that you could get without using money?
- Is there something you have that you would like to give away or trade?

Variations

1. Add small school supplies, such as pencils and erasers, to the table.
2. Take pictures of people completing their jobs and post them by the Swap Meet table.

THE TV WAY

Have you ever tried convincing four-year-olds that dinosaurs are not alive? Good luck! Today, children can see real-looking dinosaurs interacting with real people (and eating them too). Adults understand how artists create these scenes, but young children can't separate the fantasy from the reality. "Of course, it's a real dinosaur. I saw it on TV," those four-year-olds would say. And inside, they would be trembling at the thought of meeting one.

TV shows and movies can foster deep misunderstandings about reality. What happens when you get your face bashed—can you really walk away unhurt? Do "bad guys" really look and sound like the stereotyped characters children view on the screen? Is the only difference between good guys and bad guys that the good guys win? And what are girls supposed to do to feel powerful? Without our guidance, TV can provide very confusing answers to these questions.

And what about when you're scared or disagree with someone? If you believe your TV, you pick up a weapon and start blasting. Many TV shows rely on this view of the world because it's an easy way to hold children's attention.

Most toddlers can't understand the difference between TV and reality, no matter how many times an adult explains it. Children under the age of five who seem confused or scared by TV should watch it only when an adult is with them to talk about what they have seen. This is particularly true for children who cannot stop themselves from mimicking TV violence. As children get older, the Great Dinosaur Misconception will fade away, along with the idea that a cape can make you fly or a pointy stick will protect you from all evil. These fantasies can disturb adults, but they are an important part of young children's struggle to understand what is real and good in the world, and what is not. Children should be free to explore their fantasies with their whole bodies, guided by adults who model positive values and set clear safety limits. Through play, they discover what they can see, touch, smell, hear, and taste, versus what they can create inside their minds. They discover firsthand what is safe and what is not. The two-dimensional fantasy world of TV is not nearly as effective.

The TV Way isn't the same as the Real Way. This story, along with plenty of opportunities for fantasy play, will help children discover the difference as they are developmentally ready.

Use these children's books to discuss the differences between fantasy and reality and to support positive fantasy play:

Brown, Marc. *The Bionic Bunny Show.* Boston: Little, Brown and Company, 1985.

Graham, Bob. *Max.* Cambridge, Massachusetts: Candlewick Press, 2000.

Hoffman, Mary. *Amazing Grace.* New York: Dial Books, 1991.

Kroninger, Stephen. *If I Crossed the Road.* New York: Atheneum, 1997.

Ages: 4–8

WHAT IF?

Children can explore the boundary between fantasy and reality in this imagination exercise. It may start out silly, but it can foster serious discussions of what is real and what is not, especially on TV.

Materials

Directions

1. Invite a group of four to six children to play the What If game.
2. Tell the children you are going to play a game that uses their imagination.
3. Give an example of an opening line, such as "What if cars were made out of candy?" or "What if people were smaller than ants?"
4. Encourage the children to talk about and explore these possibilities.
5. Ask the children, "Could that really happen?"
6. Help the children create their own What If questions.

Discussion

These questions can be used to extend the discussion about using your imagination, so that the children can better understand how TV works:

• People have created many entertaining shows by asking "What If" questions, then writing stories about them. Can TV shows make something that is impossible look real? How do they do it?
• Can you tell what is real and what is not on a TV show? How?
• Do you ever pretend you can do things that are impossible? What are they? Why would you like to do them?

Variations

1. Ask the children to draw pictures of the imaginary scenes they create. Older children may want to write a story about a What If question. These can be collected into a What If Book.

2. Children with limited vision can record their What If questions and stories on a tape recorder.

3. Invite a children's fiction author to your class to talk about how she creates stories.

4. Invite an actor to come to your class to talk about how he pretends to be someone else.

Ages: 5–8

REWIND

How do you deal with scenes from TV and movies that leave children confused about what is real and what is not? Rewind provides an opportunity to talk about them, and a way to think of less disturbing, real-life alternatives. Once you get them started, you may be surprised by how concerned children are about some of the images they have seen.

Materials

Changing Channels CD
CD player
paper and pen

Directions

1. Invite a group of three to six children to help create a Rewind story.

2. Listen to the story "The TV Way."

3. The boy who is listening to the story on the recording keeps stopping his father to find out if the story is the Real Way or the TV Way. Ask the children if they remember what kinds of questions he asks. Listen to the story again if the children can't remember.

4. Ask a child to describe a scene that they've seen on TV, in a video, or in a movie that showed the TV Way rather than the Real Way. (For younger children, an adult may have to go first before they understand what you are requesting.) Encourage the group to discuss how they could tell the scene wasn't the Real Way. Younger children will often express their confusion with questions, such as "How come the bad guy's car crashed but he didn't get hurt?"

5. Repeat with examples brought up by other children.

6. Ask the children if they would like to Rewind one or more of the stories to make a better one, either one that is more realistic or one that is not so scary or confusing. Older children can decide as a group which scene or scenes to retell, while younger children may need an adult to select one.

7. Have everyone shout "Rewind!" and make a rewinding motion, like rewinding an old-style camera or reeling in a fishing line, along with an appropriate rewinding sound.

8. Go over the scene step-by-step, asking if the children want to change it. Write down the new story that emerges.

9. When the story is completed, read it back to the children.

Discussion

You may want to ask these questions during the activity to deepen the children's understanding of the differences between fantasy and reality:

- How can you tell the difference between the TV Way and the Real Way?
- Who gets to decide what is included in a TV show story?
- How do actors know what to do and say when they make a TV show or movie?

Variations

1. Older children will enjoy acting out scenes before and after they are rewritten. If there is any violence in a scene, ask the children to do it safely, in slow motion. Some children will even try to move in reverse while rewinding!

2. Create a Rewind Stories Book.

3. After the group has gotten used to the Rewind concept, ask the children who have broken a classroom rule if they want a chance to Rewind and try again.

CREATURES FOR THE SEASONS

Children younger than six or seven years old aren't yet developmentally able to separate the Real Way from the TV Way with any consistency. Instead, they need experience exploring their own fantasy life and their own reality. Here is a project that can help them explore both and provide an alternative to commercial "superheroes" as well. Children can create whole fantasy worlds for their characters, and learn a great deal about nature and the seasons.

Materials

scissors
white glue and glitter glue
clothespins
scraps of cloth, ribbon, and fancy paper
other small items for gluing, such as buttons, cotton balls, plastic
   jewels, and pipe cleaners
seasonal nature materials, such as flowers, seed pods, and leaves

Directions

1. At the beginning of a season, tell the children it's time to make a new doll or action figure—a Spring Fairy, a Fall Elf, a Winter Hero, or any other character they want to create. Older children may want to help you gather seasonal materials.

2. Set up four to six work stations on a covered table, with glue, scissors, markers, and a clothespin. Give the children access to gluing materials.

3. Let the children create whatever characters they would like.

4. Ask the children about their characters, and write down what they say.

5. Encourage the children to create a fantasy world for their characters in the block area or in a sand table.

Discussion

This fantasy play activity can be paired with science and family studies by asking:

- What changes happen to plants and animals when the seasons change? How does the weather change?
- How do your family's activities change with the seasons? Think about clothing, food, sports and other outdoor activities, and transportation.
- What sounds, tastes, smells, or textures do you think of when you think of the seasons?

Variations

1. Older children can use glue guns with supervision.

2. Give a group of four to six children a large piece of cardboard and items to be glued, such as sticks, colored sand, rocks, pieces of egg cartons, cotton, and small boxes. Ask them to create a world for their characters that goes with the season. Let them play with their characters in the world they create. Add small blocks, animal figures, dolls, or other materials that will enrich the play.

3. Create a book of stories about the characters for each season.

4. For children who do not have the hand-eye coordination to create small characters, use larger dolls. Make slip-on capes for the dolls by cutting circles of plain cloth with a hole in the middle for the doll's head. Use smaller circles to make simple doll hats. Let the children decorate the capes and hats with watercolors, markers, glitter glue, or fabric scraps. When dry, help the children dress the dolls and set up appropriate play materials.

Ages: 3–8

Involving Families: Family Play Dates

Family Play Dates help children see that families and teachers can work together to support their fantasy play. They also give families fun alternatives to watching TV. During a Family Play Date, teachers can model ways of supporting children's fantasy play without taking it over. They can also take the opportunity to demonstrate the ways children learn through play, and how adult attention helps children stay focused on play for longer periods of time.

Materials

letter to the families describing your Play Date (see sample below)
costumes, props, and materials to make costumes, such as old
   shirts, scarves, pieces of cloth, hats, wigs, and fake furs and jewelry
face paints and a mirror
materials to set up at your choice of play stations (examples given
   in Directions)

Directions

1. Send out a letter and survey to the families to describe Play Dates and to find out what time would work to hold a Play Date for two to three hours—evenings, weekends, or as part of the school day (see sample letter below).

2. Send an invitation to the event several weeks in advance. Be sure to invite all family members.

3. On the day of the event, set up several play stations in appropriate places that will appeal to all ages. These can include playdough, paint easels, or other art materials; a sensory table with oobleck (cornstarch and water) in it; musical instruments; a construction set such as Lego building blocks; and large floor puzzles. Be sure your activities are accessible to all who might attend.

4. In one area of your classroom or yard, set up a large area for dramatic play with costumes, props, and face paints. You may want to set up a curtain for a stage and chairs for an audience.

5. Explain to the adults that they should let their children take the lead and tell them what to do, especially if they are going to be a fantasy character. Have them ask, "What should I do next?"

6. Let everyone play! Stress that it is everybody's responsibility to make sure everyone stays safe, gets to try activities, and has their ideas included in the play.

Discussion

Here are some other issues to think about for Play Dates:

- Make sure your staff has considered the full range of ages and abilities when they choose play stations.
- Play Dates are a great time to talk to parents about the importance of fantasy play in the lives of young children, alternatives to watching TV, and the value of letting children guide adults in play on a regular basis. For more information, read *Playful Parenting* by Lawrence J. Cohen (New York: Ballantine Books, 2001) or visit the Parent Leadership Institute Web site at www.parentleaders.org.

Variations

1. Ask the families to bring snacks or food for a potluck meal.
2. If your families are interested, set up a Play Date every few months. The parents can help collect materials, set up, and clean up.
3. Hold a Play Date in a local park.

Dear Families,

At our school, we believe that children learn a lot from play. That's why we want to give you an opportunity to play with your child, during our Family Play Date event.

Sometimes it's hard for our children to get enough time with us. We might take them on errands or watch TV with them, but we may not take the time to do what they want to do—play. Our Family Play Date is a great time to set aside your routine so you can be with your child. During the event, we will set up lots of activities—art, clay, blocks, and "pretend" play—for children and adults to do together. We invite you to come and let your child be your guide. You'll have lots of fun!

Before we set up our Play Date, we want to check with you about when to hold it. Would you rather we plan the event on a weekday, during school hours? A weekday evening, with a potluck dinner? Or on the weekend, in the morning or early afternoon, with a family picnic? Please circle your preference and return this form to your child's teacher. After we find out everyone's choices, we'll let you know when to come and what to bring.

Thanks for being your child's best teacher—

- -

What times would you be able to attend a Family Play Date?

Circle as many as you wish and return to your child's teacher.

Name_____.

I would prefer to come on:

❑ A weekday from 3:00–5:00 P.M.

❑ A weekday from 6:00–8:30 P.M., with a potluck dinner

❑ A weekend from 10:00 A.M.–12:30 P.M., with a picnic lunch

❑ A weekend from 1:00–3:00 P.M.

Fostering Positive Communication and Conflict Resolution

The goal of conflict resolution with children is to get them to work out their own problems, using safe solutions that everyone agrees to. Children need to learn a lot of skills to be successful at this, so we can't expect them to be experts right away. Children must be able to stop themselves from reacting to their feelings with violence or withdrawal, express their feelings and needs in ways that others can understand, listen to the views of others, think of ideas that everyone can support, and negotiate new solutions when people don't agree—skills that are hard for many adults!

The models presented on TV and in movies don't help children learn how to solve conflicts. Children's action shows don't present realistic ways to handle fear, anger, and sadness. Characters rarely negotiate cooperative solutions—they solve most problems with weapons, brute force, and magic powers. Children who imitate these actions often believe these are the correct ways to handle their feelings. Teachers and parents must be ready to intervene to protect everyone involved.

Adults are ultimately responsible for keeping children safe, but, with a little guidance, children can be quite creative about solving their own problems. They can do their best when they are with adults who have learned to set clear limits, control and express their own feelings, listen well, and value solutions that are fair. The songs on the *Changing Channels* CD and the activities that go with them can be used to introduce many of the skills used in conflict resolution. Help children keep their cool with "Count to Ten and Try Again." Teach about the value of expressing feelings and listening to others with "Talk to Me." Emphasize the importance of avoiding violence with "Use a Word." And introduce cooperative problem solving with "Sharing."

For more ideas, check out these adult resources on feelings, cooperation, and conflict resolution with children:

Curtis, Regina. *The Little Hands Playtime Book.* Charlotte, Vermont: Williamson Publishing, 2000.

Hopkins, Susan (editor). *Hearing Everyone's Voice.* Redmond, Washington: Exchange Press, 1999. (Available through Redleaf Press.)

Levin, Diane E. *Teaching Young Children in Violent Times.* Gabriola, British Columbia, Canada: New Society Publishers, 1996.

Pelo, Ann, and Fran Davidson. *That's Not Fair!* St. Paul: Redleaf Press, 2000.

Rosenberg, Marshall B. *Nonviolent Communication.* Dell Mar, California: PuddleDancer Press, 1999. (www.puddledancer.com)

Whitehouse, Elaine. *A Volcano in My Tummy: Helping Children Handle Anger.* Gabriola, British Columbia, Canada: New Society Publishers, 1996.

COUNT TO TEN AND TRY AGAIN

5

Your friend just knocked down the airport that you spent the last half an hour building out of blocks. Your next-door neighbor says you can't come to his party. Your sister claims that your favorite ball belongs to her. What do you do? It's hard to figure out when you're overwhelmed with anger, frustration, sadness, or fear.

Many children react physically to the stress of disaster, failure, and conflict. They strike out, throw a tantrum, or run away. Others have learned to control their bodies and use words, but the words are insulting or obscene. Children may be well versed in nonviolent conflict resolution techniques, but they can't use them in real life if they can't safely discharge their emotions first. Punishing children or telling them to "Think about what you did" rarely helps, nor does pushing children to ignore their feelings just to get the problem solved quickly. What children need from us are ways to express and control their feelings, so that they can regain their ability to think and talk. And some children do need a safe, physical way to release their body tension.

Crying is one way our bodies safely release feelings, but many adults go to great lengths to stop it. For many of us, a crying child is a sign that we're not doing our job. For others, listening to crying causes great discomfort, because we were told not to "act like babies" when we were young. Our children, especially boys, have learned the same lesson. Yet many times, after children are allowed to cry, they can come up with inventive ways to resolve their situation. We can help by accepting tears as a legitimate method for expressing feelings (although not for manipulating others) and by intervening when children tease their peers for crying.

While we can't expect most older children to be comfortable with tears, "Count to Ten and Try Again" includes several other useful strategies children can learn to cope with their strong feelings, so they can move on and be creative problem solvers.

Here are some children's books you can use to help children keep their cool:

Aaron, Jane, and Barbara Gardiner. *When I'm Afraid* and *When I'm Angry.* New York: Golden Books, 1998.

Bang, Mollie. *When Sophie Gets Angry, Really, Really Angry.* New York: Scholastic, 1999.

Simon, Norma. *I Was So Mad.* Morton Grove, Illinois: Albert Whitman, 1991.

Count to Ten and Try Again

When you're feel-in' bad Or may-be just plain mad, When you want to shout or pout— A-bout the day you had, You dropped your lunch on the way to school, Your book's at the bot-tom of the swim-ming pool,— Your blocks fell in a pile,— Play it cool, real-ly cool!

oo

Count to ten and try a-gain,

It's your cool-down tool!— oo

One! Your cool-down has be-gun.— *(cool, real-ly cool)*—

Two! Don't just sit and stew. *[bubble…]*

Three! I won't let this bug me. *[bzzz…]*

By Marcy Marxer
©1996/1997 2 Spoons Music, ASCAP

Count to Ten and Try Again

by Marcy Marxer
(©1996/1997 2 Spoons Music, ASCAP)

When you're feelin' bad
Or maybe just plain mad,
When you want to shout or pout
About the day you had,
You dropped your lunch on the way to school,
Your book's at the bottom of the swimming pool,
Your blocks fell in a pile,
Play it cool, really cool!

Count to ten and try again
Count to ten and try again
Count to ten and try again
It's your cool-down tool!

One! Your cool-down has begun. *(cool, really cool)*
Two! Don't just sit and stew. *(bubble . . .)*
Three! I won't let this bug me. *(bzzz . . .)*
Four! Breathe deep and count some more.
Five! Stretch and feel alive.
Six! I've got some cool-down tricks.
Seven! Maybe help from my friend Evan. *("Hey, Evan, can you give me a hand?"*
   "Sure!")
Eight! Relax and concentrate.
Nine! I can do it this time.

Ten—Ten, try again,
Count to ten and try again.
You can do it if you play it cool, really cool.

So when you're feelin' bad or maybe just plain mad,
When you want to shout or pout about the day you had,
If you're about to lose your cool
Now you have got a cool-down tool
Don't let your nerves go wild
Play it cool, really cool!

Count to ten and try again . . .

Ages: 3–8

How Many Ways Can You Cool Down?

Everyone needs to learn cool-down techniques! "Count to Ten and Try Again" will help get people started in finding those that work for them.

Materials

Changing Channels CD
CD player
large piece of paper and marking pen

Directions

1. Listen to the song "Count to Ten and Try Again" with a group of children.

2. Ask, "What ideas in this song might help you cool down and control your feelings when you are upset?" Write down the children's answers. Examples include counting to ten, deep breathing, stretching, and asking a friend for help. Listen to the song again if the children can't remember.

3. For each idea, have the children practice the action.

4. Ask the children if they have ways to cool down that aren't mentioned in the song. Add these to your chart.

5. Post the paper in a place where the children can easily see it. When a child needs to cool down, ask, "How can I help you cool down?" Offer suggestions from the list if the child can't think of any ideas. Try to offer these ideas before the child loses control.

Discussion

These questions can help the children understand how they react to their feelings:

- Can you think of a time when you were angry or upset? How did you cool down?
- What are some of the feelings you have had that needed a cool-down period?
- Have you ever seen an adult using a cool-down tool? What was it? How did it work?

Variations

1. Create new ways to count to ten. Examples include fast or slow; loud, soft, or in silence; with claps or jumps; and backward. Have the children try out each of these ideas to see which would work best for them. See the activity Count to Ten around the World (page 72) for more ideas.

2. Ask the children to draw pictures of their feelings and write down which cool-down tool they would use or to draw themselves using a cool-down tool.

3. Show the Feelings Cards (see page 90) and ask the children which ones might require a cool-down tool.

THE COOL-DOWN SPOT

Ages: 3–8

Some children need more than a cool-down method—they need a safe place to use it. Combining the Cool-Down techniques with a Cool-Down Spot can greatly reduce the use of violence in your classroom.

Materials

large, sturdy wood or cardboard box, about 3 feet square
soft materials, such as pillows, stuffed animals, blankets, or
    carpet pieces
glue gun or staple gun
large paper and marking pen

Directions

1. Choose a quiet, out-of-the-way spot in the classroom, preferably in a corner or against a wall.

2. Place your box in the Cool-Down Spot. Create an opening, if needed. Add smaller openings for windows if the box is too dark.

3. Add the soft materials to make the space cozy. You can add cloth or carpet to the walls with the glue gun (or staple gun if you are using a wooden box).

4. Ask a group of six to eight children to help create rules for the safe use of the Cool-Down Spot. Write them down and post them nearby. Rules could include the following:

   - One person at a time.
   - Pound pillows but not walls.
   - The Cool-Down Spot is for cooling down, not for playing.
   - You can bring your own toys and blankets, but take them when you leave.

5. When children are having a conflict, and a child is too emotional to talk about it, suggest they take a few minutes in the Cool-Down Spot.

Discussion

These questions will help the children understand how to use a Cool-Down Spot:

- When would you use the Cool-Down Spot?
- How does your body feel when you need to use the Cool-Down Spot?
- How could you tell a friend that you think he or she should use the Cool-Down Spot?

Variations

1. Cool-Down Spots can also be created with small tents, blankets, and spaces under tables and inside cabinets. Be sure your Cool-Down Spot is accessible to everyone who might use it.

2. Make a separate Cool-Down Spot on your playground.

3. Older children can help design and decorate the Cool-Down Spot.

4. You can introduce the Cool-Down Spot at circle time with a doll. Use a small box to make a doll-size version of your Cool-Down Spot. Ask the children to help you make up a story in which the doll uses the spot.

Ages: 3–8   # WHOMPER

Some people can calm down with words or deep breathing, but many young children also need a safe way to release their physical tension. They can stomp their feet, pound a pillow, kick a ball . . . or use a Whomper.

Materials

dense foam rubber, about 3 inches square and 30 inches long
pillowcase or cloth bag stuffed with rags or foam pieces
rope

Directions

1. Tie one end of the rope around the stuffed pillowcase or bag. Attach the other end to a tree, fence, post, or climbing structure. Keep the rope fairly short (3 to 4 feet long, maximum); otherwise, the bag will swing around too much and the children won't be able to hit it repeatedly to release their tension.

2. Inform the children of the whomping rules. Examples include the following:
   - One person whomping at a time.
   - No fighting with whompers.
   - Whomp the target, not people or other equipment.
   - If you are whomping because you are angry at someone, once you have whomped your anger out, go solve the problem.

   Older children can help you create the safety rules that make sense for your classroom.

3. Let each child who wants to participate take a turn hitting the target with the whomper. Encourage children to put a lot of energy into their swings. After the children become accustomed to the activity, recommend it to children whose bodies are tense and angry in a conflict before they try to solve the problem.

Discussion

Keep these ideas in mind when you set up a whomping activity:
- Some children will have to observe others using the whomper before they can feel comfortable trying it.

- When you first introduce whomping, many children will want to do it for fun, so set up a system for taking turns and decide on the length of time for each turn. An egg timer will help children keep track of turns. When children are whomping because they are angry, try to give them as much whomping time as they need to calm down.
- Many children will want to turn this activity into a "swordfight." Allow one whomper at a time and talk to children about how to use it to reduce anger in order to keep the focus on cooling down.

Variations

1. Since they can break, it's a good idea to have extra whompers. Enclose the whomper in a cloth case to help keep it from tearing.

2. Swimming pool "noodles" make good whompers if you shorten them.

3. For children who need a full-body experience, attach a large piece of foam or an old mattress to a fence, wall, or sturdy tree. One at a time, let children punch, kick, and body-slam the mattress.

4. If you have children who do not have the arm strength to swing a whomper, you can modify it by attaching to a child's legs or head. Or attach a whomper to a string and pulley so the child can hit a target by pulling on the string.

5. Stomping on bubble wrap is another great way to release body tension.

6. If your classroom is in a place where you can let children make a lot of noise when they release their feelings, let them pound the whomper on empty water bottles, garbage can lids, or a big cardboard box.

INVOLVING FAMILIES: COUNT TO TEN AROUND THE WORLD

How would you count to ten if you needed to cool down in Spain? How about in Greece or Japan? Many classrooms have families that speak a variety of languages. They will enjoy helping you create this display.

Materials

paper with ten lines, numbered 1 to 10
bulletin board with space labeled Count to Ten around the World

Directions

1. Ask the families to help their child discover the numbers one to ten in a different language. The families can add languages they know, they can ask friends or neighbors, or they can find a language in a reference book or on the Internet (see examples below). Have them write the words on the lined paper, plus the name of the language. Add pronunciation guides, if available.

2. Add languages to the display as families bring them.

3. Bring one or more of the language pages to group time, or make a chart using several languages.

4. Practice counting to ten in different languages. Start with one or two that the children don't know, then add more if there is enough interest.

Discussion

Use these questions to extend the activity and help the children connect it to the idea of cooling down:

- Can you count to ten in another language when you need to cool down?
- What other words would you like to know in another language that could help you cool down?

Variations

1. To make your display area more interesting, try to find pictures from the part of the world that uses each language. Post the pictures with the words.

2. If you know someone who speaks the language, ask them to come to your group time to introduce it. Take a picture of the person to post with the language.

3. Add American Sign Language to your display (see below).

	Hmong	**Swahili**	**Spanish**	**Greek**
1	ib (ee)	moja	uno	$\varepsilon\nu\alpha$ (ena)
2	ob (aw)	mbili	dos	$\delta\upsilon o$ (dya)
3	peb (bay)	tatu	tres	$\tau\rho\iota\alpha$ (tria)
4	plaub (blau)	nne	cuatro	$\tau\varepsilon\sigma\sigma\varepsilon\rho\alpha$ (tessera)
5	tsib (gee)	tano	cinco	$\pi\varepsilon\nu\tau\varepsilon$ (pente)
6	rau (jow)	sita	seis	$\varepsilon\xi\iota$ (exi)
7	xya (shah)	saba	siete	$\varepsilon\pi\tau\alpha$ (epta)
8	yim (yee)	nane	ocho	$o\kappa\tau\omega$ (ochto)
9	cuaj (shu-ah)	tisa	nueve	$\varepsilon\nu\nu\varepsilon\alpha$ (ennia)
10	kaum (gow)	kumi	diez	$\delta\varepsilon\kappa\alpha$ (deka)

American Sign Language

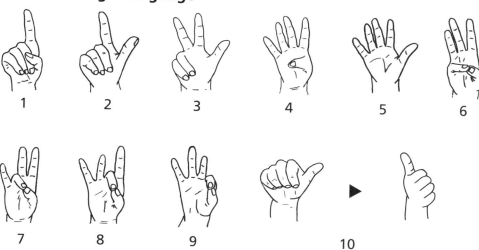

Use a Word

6

A child is upset and hurts someone with fists, or feet, or teeth. What can we do?

When young children respond to problems with violence, it may be a sign that their language is not yet developed enough to replace their need for direct, physical action. Even children who seem to have a lot of skill with words can lose those abilities under stress. But others have learned that violence is an acceptable way to communicate their needs and feelings—their anger, fear, frustration, sadness, boredom, even excitement or a desire to play. They may have picked up this misinformation from TV shows, peers, siblings, or from the adults in their lives. They may have had a lot of success in getting what they want by responding this way.

While it's important to set clear, firm limits on this violent behavior, children don't learn much from hearing "No" all the time. Since their actions are an attempt to communicate their feelings, what they learn from "No" is that their feelings are not okay. We have to offer them positive ways to problem solve so they can see that, while their behavior must change, their feelings are accepted. One of the best alternatives is to express those feelings and desires in words.

However, when children first start to use language to resolve conflicts, they often choose the most powerful words they can find—insults, threats, and swear words! Hurtful words have to be stopped too. We can recognize the progress children have made when they learn to control their physical impulses. We can offer them more appropriate language and safer ways to let out their body tension.

"Use a Word" is a great place to start children thinking about better ways to problem solve with their peers. Here are some children's books that can help, as well:

Agassi, Martine. *Hands Are Not for Hitting.* Minneapolis: Free Spirit, 2000.

Hoffman, Eric. *No Fair to Tigers.* St. Paul: Redleaf Press, 1999.

Jones, Rebecca. *Matthew and Tilly.* New York: Puffin, 1995.

Paine, Lauren Murphy. *We Can Get Along: A Child's Book of Choices.* Minneapolis: Free Spirit, 1997.

Use a Word

When some-one makes you slip And you want-a bruise their lip, Use a word. (Use a word). When some-one grabs your book And you go for your left hook, Use a word. (Use a word).

We can work it out, that's what words were in-vent-ed for, We can work it out, it's the best way there is for sure, To fight o-ver some-thing is ab-surd, So for Pete's sake, use a word.

There are so man-y diff'-rent words, they do all kinds of things, Some can make us smile and laugh while oth-ers hurt and sting, We get to choose the words we use each and eve-ry day, So when it's time to use a word be care-ful what you say.

To Chorus

By Red & Kathy Grammer
©1986 Smilin' Atcha Music, ASCAP

Use a Word

by Red and Kathy Grammer
(©1986 Smilin' Atcha Music, ASCAP)

When someone makes you slip
And you wanta bruise their lip,
Use a word. (Use a word).
When someone grabs your book
And you go for your left hook,
Use a word. (Use a word).

chorus:
We can work it out, that's what words
   were invented for,
We can work it out, it's the best way there
   is for sure,
To fight over something is absurd,
So for Pete's sake, use a word.

When someone steals your ball
And you want to make them fall,
Use a word. (Use a word).
When someone plays a trick
And you're winding up to kick,
Use a word. (Use a word).

chorus

There are so many diff'rent words, they
   do all kinds of things,
Some can make us smile and laugh while
   others hurt and sting,
We get to choose the words we use each
   and every day,
So when it's time to use a word be careful
   what you say.

chorus

When someone hurts your pride
And you want to run and hide,
Use a word. (Use a word).
When someone thinks of you
In a way that isn't true,
Use a word. (Use a word).

Everybody's different, take a look
   around and see
You're the only you I know and I'm
   the only me
Because we're all so different there'll
   be times we disagree
But I just want to say my friend that
   that's all right with me

We can work it out, that's what
   words were invented for,
We can work it out, it's the best way
   there is for sure,
To fight over something is absurd,
So for Pete's sake and Jamie's and
   Nikki's and Juan's and Jamal's and
   Debbie's and Crystal's and David's
   and Andy's
Use a word!

Ages: 3–8

THE SAFE CIRCLE

A Safe Circle chart can help children learn the difference between words that help solve problems and words that can make them worse. The song "Use a Word" provides examples of problem situations to use in your discussion of Safe Circle words.

Materials

Changing Channels CD
CD player
blank cards, about 2 by 3 inches
marking pen
circle of red paper, about 3 feet wide
circle of blue paper, about 2 feet wide
tape or tacks

Directions

1. Tape or tack the red circle to a wall. Tack the blue circle in the middle of it. Label the outer circle Danger! and the inner paper Safe.

2. Invite a group of six to eight children to help you think of safe words and unsafe words.

3. Listen to the song "Use a Word."

4. Ask the children to remember some of the conflict situations mentioned in the song. If they can't remember any, play the first verse of the song and ask what is happening in the song that could cause a fight.

5. For each conflict situation, ask the children to think of words that could help solve the problem safely, and words that might make the problem worse.

6. When a child thinks of a word or phrase, write it on an index card.

7. Ask the children whether it should go in the Safe Circle or the Danger Circle. Have a child tape or tack the card in the appropriate circle.

Discussion

While most words and phrases will fall clearly into one circle or another, the children may disagree about some, such as "Go away!" Use these questions to help the children decide:

- Do the words help solve the problem or make it worse?
- Would the words help keep everyone safe or would they be seen as an attack by one person?
- Can you say the same thing with words that are safer?

Variations

1. Have the children come up with additional conflict scenarios, and pick words from the Safe Circle that would help solve them, or add new ones.

2. Use your words from the Safe Circle in the next activity, Word Bird.

3. If you are working with children who have limited mobility, mount your circles on a larger piece of cardboard, so you can carry it to them and, if possible, allow them to attach the words. Sticky notes may be easier to use than tape or tacks.

4. With older children, look at the words in the Danger Circle and divide them into three categories: insults, threats, and anger words. For example, *chicken* is an insult; "I'm going to punch you out" and "Give it to me or you can't come to my party" are threats; and *hate* is an anger word. When children use these words at school, mention the kind of word they are using: "That word is an insult. Can you think of a safer word to solve this problem?"

Ages: 3–6

WORD BIRD

Need some words to solve a classroom conflict? It's hard to remember what to say when you're in the middle of a fight. Word Bird can come to the rescue, because she keeps safe words handy at all times.

If you've never used puppets in your classroom before, Word Bird is a great way to start. Don't worry about making up a new voice or being a professional puppeteer—young children don't need that to believe a puppet is alive.

Materials

bird puppet or stuffed animal
pad of tan or yellow sticky notes, about 3 inches square
poster board and marking pens

Directions

1. Draw a large "nest" on the poster board, as if you were looking down on it from above.

2. Introduce Word Bird at group time. Inform the children that Word Bird has decided to join the class and that she (or he) loves words. In fact, she loves them so much that she wants to make her new nest out of them. She particularly likes words that help people talk about their feelings, solve problems, or settle fights fairly and safely.

3. Ask the children to help Word Bird make her nest by thinking of words or phrases she can use. With the youngest children, an adult may have to make the first suggestion. As they come up with ideas, have Word Bird decide if the words are ones that she wants. Write any word or phrase she agrees to on a sticky note and stick it on her nest.

4. Let the children know that they can always add more words if they think of good ideas later on.

5. Find a place in your classroom for Word Bird and her nest, preferably in a spot where you can reach her easily. The nest can be tacked to the wall, and Word Bird can rest on a nearby shelf. If you use a puppet that can't stand on its own, make a support by attaching a juice can, or other tube, to a piece of wood.

6. At another group time, model how Word Bird can help the children resolve conflicts. One way to do this is to pretend that two dolls or stuffed animals are using unsafe words or actions in a conflict. Say to them, "It looks like you need help solving this problem safely. Can Word Bird help?" Have Word Bird suggest words from her nest to help the dolls talk about their feelings and the conflict. If you find that her nest doesn't have the words you need, help the children add them. Have the children practice using Word Bird to help with a variety of scenarios, such as what to do when you need to cool down, or want to play with someone, or want someone to pass you food at the table.

7. Another day, demonstrate a different way to use Word Bird. Pretend that two dolls resolve a problem safely. Have Word Bird fly over and say, "Wow! I heard you solve that problem with some great words. Can I add them to my nest?"

8. Throughout the day, when the children have disputes in the classroom, ask if Word Bird can help, or if she can use their words in her nest. Older children may be able to use Word Bird to take the role of facilitator in a conflict.

Discussion

To help the children choose words that Word Bird will accept, ask them these questions:

- Would those words help you solve a problem, or would they make it worse?
- When do you think you would use those words?
- If you were trying to solve a problem with another person, and he or she used those words, would you like it?

Variations

1. If you make your own puppet, include pockets for a note pad and pen. Add a hat that says Word Bird.

2. If you do the Safe Circle activity (see page 78), use the Safe Words in Word Bird's nest.

3. Ask the children to build a nest for Word Bird out of natural materials, then line the outside with words and have Word Bird live in it.

Ages: 3–8

Animal Talk

Children love to discover the ways animals are the same as people. Since animals can't use words, how do they tell us what they want? Older children will be able to go to a much deeper level in observing and analyzing animal communication.

Materials

set of animal pictures

Directions

1. You can create a set of animal pictures from magazine photos, calendars, drawings, or by using pictures in a book. Photos on thin papers work best when you glue them to poster board or other solid backing.
2. At group time, introduce the activity by discussing how people can use words when they are scared or angry, but animals can't.
3. Show the children the animal pictures, one at a time. Ask the children for ideas on how the animals let you know they are scared or angry. What sounds do they make? How do they move? What facial expressions do they use?

Discussion

Here are some questions that will help the children explore the topic of animal communication more deeply:

- When animals are afraid they often try to avoid a fight by running away or giving a warning signal. What can you do when you see an animal acting this way?
- When you meet a new dog, cat, or other animal, how can you tell if they are friendly? How can you let them know that you are friendly and don't mean to hurt them?
- Some people get along well with certain kinds of animals. Is that true for you? What kind of animals? How do you do it? Do you know anyone else who gets along well with animals?

Variations

1. If the children are enjoying the activity, you can expand it by asking how animals would let you know that they like you and how they might ask for food or for help.

2. Take pictures of the children while they pretend to be animals and create a display with them.

3. Create an audio tape of the sounds the children make when pretending to be animals. This is especially useful if you are working with children who have limited vision.

4. When you are outside with the children and you are near a bird or other animal, help the children notice what the animal does as you approach. What is the animal trying to tell you?

5. Ask the families to bring in pets and ask them to talk about the nonverbal signals the animals give them.

INVOLVING FAMILIES: FAVORITE WORDS

Words have many uses, especially in families. They can create or solve conflicts, transmit feelings, calm people down, or make them feel silly. Each family has its own set of favorite words. Rather than focusing only on the words families use in conflicts, this activity looks at all the words that people use to help them feel a part of their own, unique family.

Materials

clear plastic three-ring binder pages with pockets for trading cards, one for each family
white cards, cut to fit the trading-card pockets
envelopes measuring 9 by 12 inches, one for each family
marking pens
three-ring binder

Directions

1. Put one trading-card holder page in each envelope, along with enough blank cards to fill both sides and a marking pen.
2. Attach an instruction sheet to the outside of the envelope (see below).
3. Give each family an envelope to take home.
4. Decorate the front of the three-ring binder with a sign saying Our Favorite Words.
5. As the families bring in their word sheets, add them to the Favorite Words Book.
6. Bring the book to group times on a regular basis to read any new favorite words.

Discussion

Here are some questions you can ask the children to help them talk about their favorite words:

- What do you like about this word?
- Who taught you this word? Where did you hear it?
- What do you think of when you hear this word?

Variations

1. Ask the families to bring in a small family picture, or take their picture at school. Put it in one of the card pockets to help identify who brought in the words on that page.

2. Make several copies of the words. Cut the paper so that there is only one word on each slip of paper. Let the children create a word collage with them.

3. Put the words in a hat. Pick three words. Make up a story that uses these words. As children get better at making up the stories, pick more words for each story.

Dear Families,

We have been talking about words at school, words that can safely express feelings or solve problems. We would like you to help us gather more words—favorite words of your child or other family members. These can be fun words, silly words, or serious words. They can be names, places, descriptions, or things to do. They can be words that help you solve problems at home. Or they can be words that just sound interesting.

Here's how you can help. In this envelope, you will find some blank cards and a clear plastic card holder. Whenever you or your child think of a word that you want to save, write it on a card and put it in one of the card pockets. Some children think of lots of words right away, while some will take a week or more to fill up the page. When the pockets on both sides are full, put your child's name on one of the cards. Bring the page back to school, and we will put it in our Favorite Words Book.

Thanks for being your child's best teacher—

TALK TO ME

7

Children's behavior can baffle us. Why did Sam knock down his friend's blocks? Why did Laura hit her father when he came to pick her up? Why did Carlos crumple up his beautiful artwork? The emotions that these children felt just before they acted can offer us valuable clues. Children's TV shows don't explore feelings very deeply—characters get scared or angry and often react by fighting. It's up to parents and teachers to help young children be aware of the full range of their feelings and to express them safely.

Children often communicate emotions and desires with their bodies. These expressions don't always get the child what he or she really wants; sometimes they are unsafe. While it's important to set limits on unsafe behavior, you will be more effective if you also acknowledge children's underlying feelings and goals. Let them know that those feelings are acceptable, even when you are asking them to change their behavior. Then you can help them find positive ways to get what they want.

Adults often have to make their best guess about a young child's feelings. While positive feelings such as happiness and satisfaction can be easy to read, many children learn at a very young age to hide anger, fear, sadness, and frustration. It's important to check in with them about your guesses, instead of forcing your assumptions on them. When you help children label the full range of their emotions with words, you teach them that it's okay to let others know what they are feeling, and that they are not the only ones who have felt that way. You model good listening. And when children get older, you won't need to guess—they will be able to talk to you.

Use "Talk to Me" to encourage children of all ages to be aware of their feelings, to find another person who will listen to them, and to be there when their friends need them to listen. These children's books can help, as well:

Conlin, Susan. *Feelings: All My Feelings at Preschool.* Seattle: Parenting Press, 1991.

Creech, Sharon. *Fishing in the Air.* New York: HarperCollins, 2000.

Henkes, Kevin. *Wemberly Worried.* New York: Greenwillow, 2000.

Modesitt, Jeanne. *Sometimes I Feel Like a Mouse.* New York: Scholastic, 1996.

Viorst, Judith. *Alexander and the Terrible, Horrible, No Good, Very Bad Day.* New York: Atheneum, 1972.

Talk to Me

By Cathy Fink
©1996/1997 2 Spoons Music, ASCAP

Talk to Me

by Cathy Fink

(©1996/1997 2 Spoons Music, ASCAP)

There are pictures and sounds that we cannot understand,
Feelings that confuse us and you know you need a friend,
Some days we feel lucky, some days feel upside down,
Every day you know I'll be around.
So you can

Talk to me and tell me what you see
Talk to me about what you just heard
Find the words for what's inside your heart
And I'll hold you while you talk to me.

Draw for me a picture of your thoughts,
Paint for me the colors of your dreams,
There are many ways to say so many things,
And I love it when you draw for me.

This world is bigger than all of us,
Outside or even watching the TV.
A scrape upon the knee
Or something that you see,
You know that you can always come to me.

I can talk to you and tell you what I see
Talk to you about what I just heard
Find the words for what's inside my heart
And you'll hold me while I talk to you.

I'll hold you while you talk to me.

FEELINGS CARDS

Feelings Cards are a way to introduce the names of feelings and to help children see that everyone has them. This knowledge will help children become more comfortable talking about their own feelings. Use Feelings Cards with three- and four-year-olds for simple naming activities. Older groups will enjoy using the cards for storytelling.

Materials

magazines
scissors
pieces of cardboard or other backing material, about 6 by 9
  inches each
glue sticks or other adhesive
a roll of clear, wide tape or Con-Tact paper

Directions

1. Set up four to six places at a table or other suitable space. Place scissors, glue sticks, magazines, and cardboard at each station.

2. Ask the children to name feelings and give an example of a time when they felt that way.

3. Explain that you want their help in making a set of Feelings Cards for the class. Younger children may need to see an example that you have made. Ask them to find magazine pictures of people who represent these feelings. Cut them out and glue them to the cardboard pieces.

4. As the children mount their pictures, ask them to name the feeling portrayed. Write the name next to the picture. Older children may be able to do the writing themselves by copying from the list of feelings.

5. To make the cards last longer, cover them with clear tape or Con-Tact paper.

6. Before using the cards with the children, look through them to see if they represent the full spectrum of age, ethnicity, race, gender, ability, and family structures. You may have to create additional cards to achieve this balance.

7. You may need to help the children learn more complex words for their feelings. Many children have trouble going beyond "happy," "sad," or "mad." *Kids Like Us* (Redleaf Press: St. Paul, 1999) has good lists of feelings words for children two to four years old, and five to eight years old (see pages 98–99).

8. Some of the ways you can use Feelings Cards include:
   * Make up stories with the children about what happened to the people on the cards.
   * Select a feeling and ask the children to talk about times they felt that way.
   * Have each child choose a card and draw a picture to go along with it.
   * Ask the children to find more magazine pictures or to draw pictures that are examples of a feeling from one of the cards. Create a display using the pictures, drawings, and stories for that card.

Discussion

Here are some questions to ask the children to help them find pictures of feelings:

* How can you tell when a person is having a strong feeling?
* Can people have more than one feeling at the same time?
* Do babies have feelings? How about animals?

Variations

1. Some children will prefer to make their own Feelings Collage rather than individual cards.

2. You can also make Feelings Cards by taking photos of the children or by using the children's drawings.

Jack in the Box

This pretending game is a fun, safe way for children to learn how their tone of voice communicates a lot about their feelings.

Materials

cardboard or wooden box with an open top, large enough for one child to hide in but low enough for the child to climb in and out

blanket or sheet large enough to cover the top of the box

Directions

1. Ask six to eight children to play the Jack in the Box game.

2. Choose one child to be the first Jack in the Box.

3. Tell the Jack in the Box to climb in and crouch down. Cover the box with the blanket. Everyone else can sit in chairs or on mats in a large circle around the box.

4. Recite the Jack in the Box refrain. The rest of the children can join in as they memorize it:

    Jack in the Box so dark and still

    Won't you come out?

5. If the child in the box isn't ready to come out, he or she should reply:

    No, I won't! Not until

    You ask me with a _____ voice.

    The Jack in the Box can request a voice that reflects any feeling. Examples include angry, happy, sad, silly, scary, scared, tired, bored, whiny, calm, and excited.

6. Repeat the Jack in the Box refrain, using a voice that reflects the feeling requested. It's fun to get very dramatic!

7. Give the Jack in the Box two or three turns to request different voices. On the final turn, remind the Jack in the Box to pop out and say:

    Yes, I will!

8. Choose another Jack in the Box, or have the old Jack in the Box choose one, and repeat the game.

Discussion

Keep these points in mind when playing Jack in the Box:

- Children may request other kinds of voices, such as loud, soft, high, low, fast, or slow. Other voices you can use may not be associated with a particular emotion, but they're still lots of fun—try a roller-coaster voice that goes up and down and loud and soft, or a windy voice, or a fairy's voice. There are endless possibilities!
- If some children get too excited, you can control the energy by starting each new Jack in the Box with a calm, quiet voice, or by asking everyone to use a cool-down method between turns (see How Many Ways Can You Cool Down, page 66).

Variations

1. If you have children in your group who are unable to climb into a box or say the rhyme, modify the game for the whole group. For example, put a blanket over the children where they sit instead of having them get in a box, or have the children select a response from a set of Feelings Cards and then have an adult say the response.

2. Add animal voices. For example, a cat might say:

   Meow me-me-meow me-meow meow meow

   Meow me-me-meow?

   And the child would reply:

   Meow meow meow! Meow me-meow

   Me-meow meow meow a meow.

3. Jack in the Box can also be played as a guessing game. When the child in the box requests a voice, silently choose one child to reply. The Jack in the Box has to guess who responded and gets another turn if correct.

4. A large group can play a miniature Jack in the Box game. Show everyone how to fold their hands with one of their thumbs hidden inside. Give each child a turn to pick a voice. Every few turns, have everyone shout, "Yes, I will!" and pop their thumbs out.

TALK TO ME DOLLS

Children who are not comfortable talking to other people about their feelings may be able to get started by talking to a doll instead.

Materials

large doll or stuffed animal, different from any other in the classroom
small unbreakable mirror

Directions

1. Set up a small table and chair or other comfortable spot in a quiet corner of the room. Label it the Listening Place.

2. If possible, attach the mirror to the doll, either on the doll's chest or in its hands.

3. Introduce the Talk to Me Doll at group time. Let the children know that the doll isn't for play, but will always be at the Listening Place to listen to whatever anyone has to say. One way to introduce the Talk to Me Doll is to pretend that a puppet or another doll has something they want to talk about, but is too embarrassed or shy to do it. Let the puppet know they can share their feelings with the Talk to Me Doll. Have children suggest what they might say.

4. Leave the Talk to Me Doll at the Listening Place at all times. When children seem to have unexpressed feelings that are troubling them, suggest (but don't require!) that they sit with the Talk to Me Doll.

Discussion

The children may take a little time to become comfortable with the Talk to Me Doll. You can help by talking for the doll at first, asking such questions as:

- How are you feeling? (If you are fairly certain of the emotion, you can help by naming it: "You look sad to me. Are you feeling sad?")
- Can you tell me what happened?
- What do you think you should do?
- Who else would you like to talk to?

Variations

1. If you feel comfortable using puppets, create a Talk to Me Puppet. Young children will often talk to a puppet on your hand, even when they won't talk to you.

2. Add a tape recorder to the Listening Place.

3. If children are more comfortable expressing their feelings through art, encourage them to show their work to the Talk to Me Doll and to tell the doll a little about their picture. Or bring the doll over to the art table.

4. Do your Talk to Me Doll's physical characteristics reflect the diversity of children in your classroom? You may want to have several Talk to Me Dolls. Label each with a name and offer children a choice.

Involving Families: Memories

Children need to see that talking about feelings is also important for adults—both at school and at home. A book of Memory Stories from family members can help children make that connection.

Materials

place in the room where the adults can sit and write
story forms on preprinted, three-hole-punched papers (see sample below)
letter explaining the Memory Project (see sample below)
pens or other writing tools
tape recorder and blank tape
three-ring binder

Directions

1. Send a Memory Project letter to every family.

2. Set up a comfortable writing place where the children can watch the adults write. Include pens, story forms, and a tape recorder for those who can't write or prefer to dictate their stories.

3. Post a copy of the instruction letter nearby.

4. Decorate the front of the binder with a sign that says Memory Stories, or Stories about Our Feelings.

5. Invite all family members to participate. Show them the story forms and go over how to use them. They can write the name of the feeling on the first line to complete the title (for example, "When I Felt Sad and Confused"), and their name and relationship to a child in the line below it ("By Melissa Gordon, Aaron's grand-mother"). If they can't remember their age at the time, ask them to make their best guess.

6. As people write their stories, add them to the binder. You may also want to post new stories on a display for a few days before putting them in the binder.

7. Read the stories to the children whenever they are interested.

Discussion

Many adults have had negative experiences with writing at school, so they may be reluctant to participate. To get this project off the ground, try these ideas:

- Make personal contact with the families to explain the project and find out who is most willing to participate.
- Point out the tape-recording option. Let people know that a staff member can write the story from the tape.
- Post several examples of stories on a display nearby to help people get started. Staff can contribute the first ones. Be sure the samples are simple and short, cover a range of emotions, and do not tell stories that are embarrassing or revealing of information that people might consider too private.
- Remind them that they can take copies of the story form home if they are more comfortable working there. If they don't want to participate, perhaps someone else in the family would like to.

Variations

1. Ask each adult who completes a story to bring in a current picture, plus one from the time of the story. Mount the photos on paper and protect them inside a clear plastic sleeve, then add to the binder after the story.

2. The children can add their own Memory Stories. They may want to draw a picture first, then dictate the story to an adult.

3. Read some of the stories at group time. Some adults may be willing to come in to read their own story and answer questions about it.

   To make forms for Memory Project stories, type this information at the top of a page and copy it:

   When I Felt _____

   By _____

   A memory from when I was _____ years old:

(Leave the rest of the page blank for people to write their stories.)

A sample letter explaining the Memory Project:

Dear Families,

Our class has been talking about feelings. You can help us by telling us a short story from your childhood.

Can you remember a time when you had a strong feeling? What happened that made you feel that way? Were you sad, happy, angry, frustrated, excited?

We have a table in our writing center where you can sit and write your story or dictate it into a tape recorder. We will add your story to our Memories Book.

Anyone is welcome to participate: parents, brothers and sisters, grandparents, roommates, friends. We prefer that you write your story here at school. When the children see a variety of people writing, they are more likely to be interested in learning to write. However, if you can't, feel free to take copies of our story forms home with you to fill out.

Thanks for being your child's best teacher—

SHARING

8

"Let's share!"

What does that mean to young children? It could mean:

"Let's take turns."

"Go away. I'll give it to you when I'm done."

"I know a game that we can play together."

"This is for everyone, not just you."

"I want to be your friend."

"I'm not your friend, so give it to me and go play someplace else."

"Can I join this game?"

"I want to play with you, but I don't want anyone else to play with us."

"I don't know what to do, but I know what adults like to hear."

Some of these statements are from children who understand that fair solutions take everyone's needs into account. Others reveal an egocentric state of mind. So when children offer sharing as a solution to a social problem, teachers have to listen carefully and observe body language, facial expressions, tone of voice, and context to be able to clarify each child's intent. And when adults tell children to share, they shouldn't assume that everyone knows what they are talking about.

Sharing, and other forms of compromise, can help preschoolers solve a basic predicament: they want to be in charge, but they want friendships too. That's hard to do when your friends also want to be in charge. Children can get stuck believing that there is never enough in the world for them. Sharing helps everyone get what they need; figuring that out is a major milestone in children's social development.

But children won't learn much if sharing is forced on them. Adults can facilitate their learning by giving them opportunities to create their own sharing plans, and by talking about the many ways to share, even at times when there is no conflict to solve. The song "Sharing" is a great way to introduce the idea that the best solutions help everyone feel like a winner—that together is better!

Here are some children's books that focus on sharing and cooperation:

Cyrus, Kurt. *Slow Train to Oxmox*. New York: Farrar, Straus and Giroux, 1998.

Hoberman, Mary Ann. *One of Each*. Boston: Little, Brown and Company, 2000.

Lionni, Leo. *It's Mine*. New York: Crown, 1996.

Root, Phyllis. *One Duck Stuck*. Cambridge, Massachusetts: Candlewick Press, 1998.

Stadler, John. *One Seal*. New York: Orchard, 1999.

SHARING

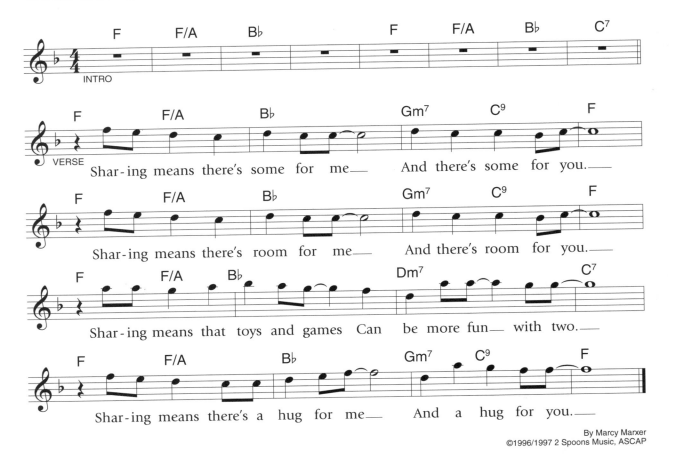

Shar-ing means there's some for me___ And there's some for you.___

Shar-ing means there's room for me___ And there's room for you.___

Shar-ing means that toys and games Can be more fun___ with two.___

Shar-ing means there's a hug for me___ And a hug for you.___

By Marcy Marxer
©1996/1997 2 Spoons Music, ASCAP

Sharing

by Marcy Marxer

(©1996/1997 2 Spoons Music, ASCAP)

Sharing means there's some for me
And there's some for you.
Sharing means there's room for me
And there's room for you.
Sharing means that toys and games
Can be more fun with two.
Sharing means there's a hug for me
And a hug for you.

Ages: 4–8

GIFTS FROM THE EARTH

Sharing is an issue that often comes up when children are fighting over toys, but children can learn a great deal about sharing when there is no conflict. Here is a simple sharing ritual, followed by craft activities, to help children see that we share a world larger than the one we have set up with our possessions. There are many Gifts from the Earth to share, and people are one of them.

Materials

Changing Channels CD
CD player
a bowl and a bag (or other containers) for each child
Gifts from the Earth—herbs, fresh or dried flowers, pinecones or other seed pods, small pieces of driftwood or branches, small rocks, shells, feathers, or potpourri mixtures

Directions

1. Gather several kinds of Gifts from the Earth. The children can help with this step if you have a garden, woods, meadow, or other safe gathering spot near your school. Keep different materials in separate containers.

2. Make sure you have enough so every child can have some of each kind. If necessary, cut materials into smaller pieces.

3. Listen to the song "Sharing" with your group.

4. Give each child a bowl with one type of Gift from the Earth in it. If you have a large group, several children may have bowls with the same kind of gift in it.

5. Tell the children that they each have one kind of Gift from the Earth, but that you would like everyone to share all the gifts.

6. Give each child a bag.

7. Play the song again. While the music is playing, have the children take turns putting pieces of their gift into the other children's bags.

8. Ask the children for ideas about what they could do with their gifts. Ideas include the following:
   - wrap them as a gift for someone else
   - make a collage

- create herb sachet necklaces
- make table decorations (Use a handful of old playdough or clay on a cardboard base. Decorate with dried flowers, feathers, and pieces of evergreen twigs up to 6 inches long.)
- build a bird's nest inside strawberry baskets

Discussion

Use these questions to stimulate more discussion about sharing Gifts from the Earth:

- What else is a Gift from the Earth?
- What are other ways to share these gifts?
- Do we share these gifts only with people? Can we share them with other animals too?
- What is your favorite Gift from the Earth? How would you share it with others?
- Are you a Gift from the Earth?

Variations

1. Let the children gather whatever materials for gifts they want, or bring some from home. Ask them to put any gifts they are willing to share into a large bowl or basket. Let anyone take whatever he or she needs, leaving enough for others. Help the children keep the bowl replenished.

2. To focus on a sensory experience, or for children with limited vision, gather materials that have pleasant smells. While freshly gathered herbs and flowers work well, you can also use spices, citrus peels, garlic, and other materials with strong smells. Make a set of smell bags out of netting and use the different materials you were able to collect.

Ages: 3–8

TIRE PULL

Sharing can mean working together to reach a goal. Tire Pull is a very physical way to teach children about this kind of sharing.

Materials

old tires
rope
tape, chalk, traffic cones, flags, or other ways to mark off a path

Directions

1. Tie the old tires together with rope. Use enough tires so that one child can't move them alone—two is usually enough for three-year-olds, more for older children.

2. Tie extra lengths of rope, about 5 feet long, to the tires.

3. Mark off a pathway on the playground. Try to cover a variety of surfaces: sand, grass, dirt, asphalt. Make sure the path is wide enough for the tires and a group of children. You may want to include one or more turns in the path.

4. Ask three to six children to work together to pull the tire from one end of the path to the other. Some will want to pull from the front, and some will want to push.

5. Supervise the activity closely to watch for collisions or children who are getting tangled.

6. Add or take away tires as needed to make the task challenging but not impossible.

Discussion

These questions will help the children think about some of the issues behind this very physical activity:

- If someone falls down or gets stuck, what signal should let everyone know to stop?
- Before people had powerful machines, how did they move heavy objects or build tall buildings?
- What happens when everyone pulls in different directions?

Variations

1. Add more challenges to the path by having the children go up a hill, a climbing structure, or other obstacle.

2. Let the children take turns riding on the tires while the rest of the group pulls.

3. Older children can help figure out how to tie the tires together.

4. If you have children who use wheelchairs or other mobility devices, help them decide how they can safely participate. For example, the children who use wheelchairs may want to tie ropes onto their equipment and participate in a small group. Be sure that the pathway goes over surfaces that are accessible.

THE CITY

We also share a community with homes, roads, stores, and other structures. Children can learn more about sharing a community by creating their own, together!

Materials

small boxes of different shapes and sizes
masking tape and/or duct tape
marking pens
scissors
permanent marker

Directions

1. Mark off a "roadway" with tape on a large concrete, linoleum, or asphalt surface. Make the road large enough for the children to walk on, about 3 feet wide (5 feet wide if you have children who use mobility equipment).

2. Ask the children to make houses and other buildings for the street by decorating boxes. They can use markers to decorate them, scissors to make openings, and tape to hold boxes together. Tape buildings down along the roadway. Younger children may need adult help to cut openings in the boxes, and to cut the tape.

3. Ask the children what kinds of structures they are creating. Help them label their stores, libraries, office buildings, and so forth. Older children may want to add addresses.

4. Let the children add new roadways as the city grows. Help them name the streets and make street signs.

Discussion

Ask the children these questions after they have spent some time building their city:

- In a real city, who gets to decide what kinds of buildings get built? Who decides where the streets go? Who names them?
- What kinds of workers, tools, and materials are needed to build a real house? An office building? A road?

Variations

1. The children can add people by drawing them or cutting out magazine pictures, then attaching them to blocks of wood.

2. Give the children small vehicles to drive through their city.

3. As the community expands, the children can add parking lots; playgrounds with equipment made out of sticks; lakes and rivers of blue cloth; gardens; a post office and mail boxes with mail to deliver; traffic signs and stop lights; and bus stops.

4. This activity can be modified to reflect whatever type of community you live in—rural, urban, or suburban.

Ages: 3–8

INVOLVING FAMILIES: QUILT MURALS

There are many ways to share. Quilts allow people to work on their own piece of a project, and then discover that, when everyone puts their pieces together, something new and marvelous is created.

Materials

white paper, about 9 inches square
marking pens, crayons, or colored pencils
envelopes, about 10 by 12 inches

Directions

1. Make four to six packets, each with about ten paper squares and a set of pens, crayons, or pencils. Use the large envelopes to hold them.

2. Tape directions for the project onto the outside of the envelope. For example:

   Thank you for participating in our quilt mural, a cooperative art project created by all our families. Please use the enclosed paper squares and pens to draw pictures or designs for the mural. You can make as many as you like! We encourage all your family members to contribute.

   Bring your drawings to your child's teacher, and she will add them to the mural. Look for it on the hall bulletin board and watch it grow!

   When you are done with this quilt packet, please return it so that other families can participate.

3. Create a bulletin board or wall space for the quilt mural. The mural may start out small, but it can get very large over time—so leave plenty of room!

4. Place the art packets on a nearby table, along with a sign-out sheet. You can also have additional art materials at the table, so family members can create squares at school.

5. Point out and explain the activity to the families over the next few days, and ask them to participate.

6. As the families bring in their squares, add them to the mural, using tape.

Discussion

For children who show an interest in the quilt concept, here are some questions that can expand their understanding:

- Have you ever seen a real quilt? How do people work together to make them? Bring in an example to share.
- Is there a way to make a quilt mural using other shapes, besides squares? A set of patterns or parquetry blocks can help children discover what other shapes will work.
- How big do you think the quilt mural will grow?

Variations

1. Ask the families to make pictures using a particular design element or focusing on one topic. Examples:
   - Decorated handprints
   - Designs using shades of one color
   - Designs using at least one circle
   - What I did this summer
   - My wish for peace
   - My favorite animal

2. Have the children work in pairs to create squares.

3. Use squares of white cloth instead of paper. Post them on a board, or sew them into a blanket, banner, or flag.

SUPPORTING CHILDREN'S SELF-ESTEEM

We want our children to be able to resist the negative influences of media, resolve conflicts without violence, and work cooperatively in our classrooms. These skills become easier to learn and use when children feel good about who they are. While classroom activities that support positive self-regard do not guarantee that children will develop these skills, they set the groundwork for success.

Many people try to raise children's sense of worth by focusing on how they are each unique and special. That's one element of self-esteem, but there are other important parts that need our support. Our individual lives depend on a web of interwoven relationships, and our families, peers, and community have a great influence on how we see ourselves. Without a recognition of our similarity and connection to other people (and to all living things), pride in our families and cultures, and a hopeful vision of the future, high self-esteem can become cynical egotism.

This section of the book includes activities that can help children create mutually supportive friendships, develop a sense of community, recognize the dignity of every family, and learn how to care for others. "That's What I Like about You" will help children discover what's best in themselves, their friends, their school, and their families. "The Power in Me" focuses on ways children can use their power to help others. "A Ballet Dancing Truck Driver" looks at ways to give children a positive vision of all that children and adults can do in the world. These are all essential components of any self-esteem curriculum.

For more information on self-esteem, caring, and community, try these resources from Redleaf Press:

Hewitt, Deborah, and Sandra Heidemann. *The Optimistic Classroom*. St. Paul: Redleaf Press, 1998.

Oehlberg, Barbara. *Making It Better*. St. Paul: Redleaf Press, 1996.

Rice, Judith Anne. *The Kindness Curriculum*. St. Paul: Redleaf Press, 1997.

Ross, Kate. *Help Yourself!* (based on the CD *Help Yourself!* by Cathy Fink and Marcy Marxer). St. Paul: Redleaf Press, 2001.

York, Stacey. *Roots and Wings*. St. Paul: Redleaf Press, 1991.

A Ballet Dancing Truck Driver

9

"You can't be a firefighter—you're a girl!"

"I'm a boy, so I can't be the nurse. I have to be the doctor."

Where do these "facts" come from? Young children are constantly observing the world, trying to make sense of it. They gather information from any source available—family, friends, teachers, TV, music, even strangers—and make their best guess about how their culture works. Preschoolers are notorious for making grand judgments based on a few facts, but they don't have the skill to determine which facts are reliable and which should be ignored.

TV and movies, in particular, can expand the world tremendously by presenting people and places that children would never otherwise see. Some shows take this power seriously and do an admirable job of representing human diversity. But many others are content to reinforce gender, race, and other stereotypes—the lazy way to develop characters. If these stereotypes go unchallenged, or are reinforced by the real world, then young children will accept them and use them to limit themselves and others. By mid-elementary school, these pre-prejudices may harden into unquestioned beliefs.

So how do you change a four-year-old's opinion? Remember that their ideas are usually accurate descriptions of what they've seen and heard in their lives. They are rarely swayed by adult lectures, but they are wide open to change based on new experiences. So the best way to counteract misinformation and pre-prejudice is to provide new experiences that present a broader view of people's possibilities. Bring a male nurse into your classroom, or a female firefighter, or a ballet dancing truck driver. Play the song and try some of the activities. Then give the children time to use their intelligence. A month later, you might hear, "I'm a girl. Of course I can be a firefighter!"

If you're looking for books about workers that don't reinforce stereotypes, try these:

Grimes, Nikki. *Shoe Magic.* New York: Orchard, 2000.

Johnson, Dolores. *My Mom is Show and Tell.* Tarrytown, New York: Marshall Cavendish, 1999.

Maynard, Christopher. *Jobs People Do.* New York: DK Publishing, 2001.

Rockwell, Anne F. *Career Day.* New York: HarperCollins, 2000.

Rylant, Cynthia. *Mr. Grigg's Work.* New York: Orchard, 1993.

Spinelli, Eileen. *Boy, Can He Dance!* New York: Aladdin, 1997.

A Ballet Dancing Truck Driver

1. One day my grand-ma asked me, What do you want to be? I thought and thought and thought some more, I want to be a truck driv-er. (I want to be a truck driv-er.)

8. I looked up at the moon And now I want to be An as-tro-naut— Lift Off! A math teach-er— 2 and 2 is 4, A car-pen-ter nail-ing— tap, tap, tap, The fin-est cook— Soup's on! — An el-e-phant tam-er— Sit here, please! A run-ner rac-ing— Read-y, Set, Go! And a bal-let danc-ing truck driv-er. (A bal-let danc-ing truck driv-er.)

* In succeeding verses, add the appropriate two-measure segment here, accumulating up to verse 8 (given above).

By Marcy Marxer
©1996/1997 2 Spoons Music, ASCAP

A Ballet Dancing Truck Driver

by Marcy Marxer

(©1996/1997 2 Spoons Music, ASCAP)

One day my grandma asked me,
"What do you want to be?"
I thought and thought and thought some
    more,
I want to be a truck driver.
(I want to be a truck driver.)

But as I was watching TV
I thought ballet's the dance for me
So now I know I want to be
A ballet dancing truck driver.
(A ballet dancing truck driver.)

Then I saw the Olympics
So now I want to be
A runner racing—Ready, Set, Go!
And a ballet dancing truck driver.
(A ballet dancing truck driver.)

Then we went to the circus
So now I want to be
An elephant tamer—Sit here, please!
A runner racing—Ready, Set, Go!
And a ballet dancing truck driver.
(A ballet dancing truck driver.)

Then we went to a restaurant
So now I want to be
The finest cook—Soup's on!
An elephant tamer—Sit here, please!
A runner racing—Ready, Set, Go!
And a ballet dancing truck driver.
(A ballet dancing truck driver.)

I saw a new construction site
So now I want to be
A carpenter nailing—tap, tap, tap,
The finest cook—Soup's on!
An elephant tamer—Sit here, please!
A runner racing—Ready, Set, Go!
And a ballet dancing truck driver.
(A ballet dancing truck driver.)

But I really do love numbers
And so I'd like to be
A math teacher—2 and 2 is 4,
A carpenter nailing—tap, tap, tap,
The finest cook—Soup's on!
An elephant tamer—Sit here,
    please!
A runner racing—Ready, Set, Go!
And a ballet dancing truck driver.
(A ballet dancing truck driver.)

I looked up at the moon
And now I want to be
An astronaut—Lift Off!
A math teacher—2 and 2 is 4,
A carpenter nailing—tap, tap, tap,
The finest cook—Soup's on!
An elephant tamer—Sit here,
    please!
A runner racing—Ready, Set, Go!
And a ballet dancing truck driver.
(A ballet dancing truck driver.)

One day my grandma asked me,
"What do you want to be?"
I said, "I don't know! There are so
    many interesting things to be!"
She said, "That's okay! You have
    plenty of time to decide.
And besides, you have lots of good
    ideas! Like—"

An astronaut—Lift Off!
A math teacher—2 and 2 is 4,
A carpenter nailing—tap, tap, tap,
The finest cook—Soup's on!
An elephant tamer—Sit here,
    please!
A runner racing—Ready, Set, Go!
And a ballet dancing truck driver.
(A ballet dancing truck driver.)

LET'S PRETEND

Children enjoy moving to music. There are many possibilities for movement in "A Ballet Dancing Truck Driver."

Materials

Changing Channels CD
CD player

Directions

1. Listen to the song "A Ballet Dancing Truck Driver" with a group of children. Use a space that is large and safe enough for whole-body movement.

2. Ask the children to remember the jobs that are mentioned in the song. If the group can't remember all of them, listen to the song again.

3. Create motions to go along with each occupation in the song. For example:

   - truck driver—hold onto a steering wheel and drive, making an engine sound.
   - ballet dancing truck driver—drive with your steering wheel, but add ballet moves, such as twirls or jumps.
   - runner—pretend to start a race while saying, "Ready, Set, Go!" Get on all fours, low to the ground (Ready); then on all fours with body raised (Set); then Go!
   - elephant tamer—raise a wand as if commanding elephants to sit while saying, "Sit here, please!" Some children may want to be the elephants and make elephant sounds.
   - cook—stir a big pot of soup while saying, "Soup's on!"
   - carpenter—hammer a nail while making a tap-tap sound.
   - math teacher—hold up two fingers on one hand, then two on the other hand, then four fingers on one hand, while saying, "Two and two is four."
   - astronaut—blast off in your rocket ship while saying, "Lift Off!"

4. Practice the motions until everyone has learned them.

5. Listen to the song again, this time adding the motions. It's hard to keep up with the song by the end!

Discussion

- Do you know anyone who does a job mentioned in the song?
- Which of the jobs in the song interest you the most?
- Can a person be interested in more than one job, like a ballet dancing truck driver?

Variations

1. Have each child choose one of the jobs, then take their turn when their occupation comes up in the song. Each child could create a costume or other props for his or her job.

2. Think of additional jobs to add and make up motions for them.

3. Call out an occupation and have the children make the motions that go along with it. Keep calling out jobs from your list. Start slowly, and get faster, until the children can barely keep up!

Ages: 5–8

HOW DO PEOPLE HELP EACH OTHER?

We can't live without the support of the many people around us who are doing their jobs. This exercise looks at how we get what we need with the help of others' work.

Materials

set of pictures that illustrate people meeting their basic needs for food, clothing, shelter, friendship, transportation, education, and health
large papers and a marking pen

Directions

1. Create your set of pictures from magazines, calendars, photos, or drawings. Be sure your pictures cover the diversity of people and their needs. You may want to mount thin paper on cardboard or some other sturdy backing.

2. Show one of the pictures to a group of six to eight children. Ask the children to tell you what the person in the picture is doing—eating, getting dressed, and so on.

3. Explain that we all rely on other people to help us meet our needs, and that you want everyone to think about the kinds of jobs people do that would help the person in the photo. Use the first photo as an example to help the children understand what you are asking for. For a picture of a child eating, you could mention farmers, food pickers, truck drivers, grocers, cooks, and parents. For a person in a hospital taking some medicine, the list could include doctors, nurses, pharmacists, and ambulance drivers.

4. For each picture, ask the children to help you make a list of the related jobs.

Discussion

Use these questions to enrich the discussion of how people help each other:

• Have you ever done what the person in the picture is doing? Were there people who helped you?

- Have you ever helped someone take care of this need? How did you help?
- For each job the children think of, ask them if they have ever met anyone who does that job.
- Which of these jobs would you be interested in doing?

Variations

1. Make a bulletin-board display for one of the basic needs. Find pictures to illustrate all of the related occupations, or ask children to draw pictures. You can also add photos of how staff and the children help each other with that basic need. For example, for a health display, you can include pictures of a child helping another child put on a bandage and a group of children washing their hands.

2. Create a fantasy play for one of the basic needs, along with props that would allow the children to pretend to be any of the related occupations.

3. Ask the children to think of a person who has helped them. Write or draw thank-you notes to those people.

WHAT I CAN BE COLLAGE

We want our children to have a positive vision for their future. While most children aren't ready to make decisions about what they will do as adults, this collage project can help them understand they have a lot of choices available to them.

Materials

magazines
construction paper
scissors
glue sticks, tape, or other glue

Directions

1. Cover a table with a plastic cloth. Set up four to six chairs at the table. Put scissors and glue at each spot. Place the construction paper and magazines in the middle. Be sure the magazines portray a wide variety of people and jobs.

2. Let the children choose magazines and construction paper. Ask them to look through the magazines for pictures that show people working or helping others. Have them cut out the pictures of activities they might like to do.

3. Ask each child to glue their pictures on a piece of construction paper.

4. If they would like, the children can dictate the names of jobs or other information about the pictures, and you can write it down on their paper.

Discussion

As the children are working on their collages, you can get a discussion started with one or more of these questions:

- Do you know anybody who does that job?
- What would you need to learn to do that kind of work?
- What tools would you need?
- How does that job help people?

Variations

1. Make a list of tools used by each job.

2. Older children can choose one of the occupations from their collage and draw a picture or dictate a story about themselves doing that job.

3. Invite to your classroom people from the community who perform some of the jobs on your collages. In particular, bring in people whose work will challenge some of the gender stereotypes children may hold—a woman construction worker or police officer, a male nurse or stay-at-home parent.

Ages: 3–8

Involving Families: Hobby and Job Sharing Days

Children are always interested in classroom visitors who show them the work they do. Your families probably have a wide variety of interests—why not invite them in? Make a special effort to invite those who can break stereotypes your children may hold.

Materials

letter to the families asking them to participate in Hobby and Job Sharing Days (see below)

Directions

1. Send a copy of the letter to each family. Follow up with personal contact, if possible.

2. As the parents respond, set up a schedule of presentations, no more than one a day. Find out what props they will bring, whether the children can participate or just watch, what kind of setup will work best for them, whether they want you to help explain what they are doing, and any safety rules the children should know.

3. Early in the day of each presentation, let the children know what will happen and help them formulate questions: "Today, Alena's mother will be coming in to show us some of her carpentry tools. She said she would bring her hammer, her saw, and her drill. We'll have her presentation outside after snack. Can you think of any questions you might ask her? Let's write them down."

4. Have the children help arrange the area for the presentation, if possible.

5. Before the presentation begins, let the children know how they can participate. Go over any rules and expectations you have for the children's behavior.

6. After the presentation, ask the children to create a thank-you note.

Discussion

Here are some points to remember that will help the children get more out of the presentations:

- Children are usually very interested in other families and what they do. One area where you can focus discussion is on the concepts of *same* and *different*—a visitor may have an interest or a family structure that is the same as yours, or she may have an interest that you don't share. Both of these alternatives can be fun to talk about.

- Ask some of your presenters to talk about how they have used their interest to help others, and how it makes them feel about themselves.

Variations

1. Take pictures of each presentation, if possible. Create a bulletin board of the pictures and any other materials that are appropriate. Send a copy of the picture with the thank-you note.
2. Take field trips to visit family members at work or at play. Be sure that the environment is safe for your age group before you go.

A sample letter for Hobby and Job Sharing Days:

Dear Families,

Our class is busy learning about all the ways adults take care of themselves, their families, and others in our community. Our best examples come from the families in our classroom. We would like you to help us by sharing what you do in your job, volunteer work, or hobby.

Our first choice would be for you or someone else in your family to come to our classroom and bring something interesting to share with the children. Young children don't need elaborate descriptions, just something simple to watch—a tool you use, an example of something you make or do or are learning about, or anything else that you could demonstrate. However, we know that not every family can come in during the day, so we would be happy to show the children materials you send in—photos, tape recordings, written descriptions, or videos.

Over the next few weeks, we'll be checking in with you to see how you might be able to participate and how we can help.

Thanks for being your child's best teacher—

THAT'S WHAT I LIKE ABOUT YOU

10

Most children are very sensitive to the opinions of others. Children build their self-image by combining what they know about themselves with what they hear from people around them. It's hard to keep a positive outlook about yourself when the world keeps putting you down!

Many of us grew up with adults who pointed out everything we did wrong. How often do we remember to tell our own children what we like about them? While children need realistic feedback from us when their behavior doesn't meet our expectations, it's easy to forget that they also need to hear what they do well.

However, praise can backfire. A child who is overly praised can grow up expecting it as a reward, with little inner motivation. The wrong kind of praise can also be detrimental. Girls, in particular, often get admired for their looks or for the clothes they wear, while boys are complimented on what they can do. Many well-intentioned teachers talk only about appearances when greeting children. A child may decide that she has to hide her true self, which is not always neat and pretty, and present only a beautiful facade to the world.

You can help children feel good about themselves by noticing what they have learned or accomplished and by helping them notice the positive aspects of the people and the community around them. Straightforward statements that show you are paying attention to their efforts can have a greater impact than a thousand words of overly sweet, sweeping praise. "That's What I Like about You" can give you good examples of simple, specific observations that focus on children's actions and attitudes.

Here are some books you can use when talking about what is positive about each child and family, your classroom, your neighborhood, and your world:

Brown, Tricia. *Someone Special Just Like You.* New York: Henry Holt, 1984.

Bunnett, Rochelle. *Friends at School.* New York: Star Bright Books, 1996.

Carlson, Nancy L. *I Like Me!* New York: Viking, 1988.

Gainer, Cindy. *I'm Like You, You're Like Me.* Minneapolis: Free Spirit, 1998.

Kuklin, Susan. *How My Family Lives in America.* New York: Simon and Schuster, 1992.

Thomas, Shelly. *Somewhere Today: A Book of Peace.* Morton Grove, Illinois: Albert Whitman, 1998.

Tʜᴀᴛ's Wʜᴀᴛ I Lɪᴋᴇ ᴀʙᴏᴜᴛ Yᴏᴜ

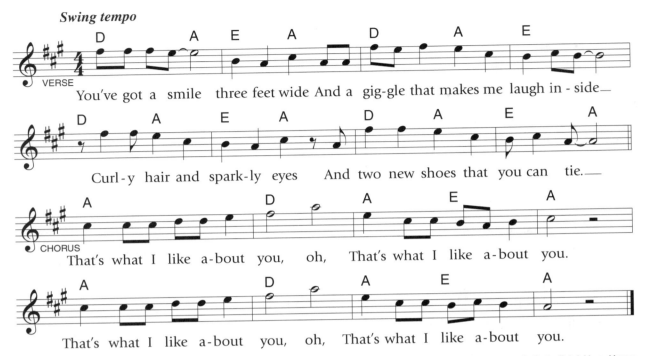

Swing tempo

VERSE
You've got a smile three feet wide And a gig-gle that makes me laugh in-side

Curl-y hair and spark-ly eyes And two new shoes that you can tie.

CHORUS
That's what I like a-bout you, oh, That's what I like a-bout you.

That's what I like a-bout you, oh, That's what I like a-bout you.

By Cathy Fink & Marcy Marxer
©1996/1997 2 Spoons Music, ASCAP

That's What I Like about You

by Cathy Fink & Marcy Marxer
(©1996/1997 2 Spoons Music, ASCAP)

You've got a smile three feet wide
And a giggle that makes me laugh inside
Curly hair and sparkly eyes
And two new shoes that you can tie.

chorus:
That's what I like about you, oh,
That's what I like about you. (2X)

I like the way you share your toys
With all the other girls and boys
I like the way that you say, "Hi!"
When someone new is walking by.

chorus

When someone's sad and feelin' blue
You seem to know just what to do
You talk to them and hold their hand
To let them know they've got a friend.

chorus

When it was your turn up at bat
You struck out and that was that
You didn't pout or sit and cry
You gave it another good old try.

chorus

When someone goofs or trips and falls
Or answers wrong or can't recall
You never laugh or nag or tease
But give them help to feel at ease.

chorus

TALKING AND LISTENING STICKS

Many children need a structured way to talk about what they appreciate in others. Talking and Listening Sticks provides a confidence-building tool to help children to speak and a way for children to practice the important skill of listening.

Materials

Changing Channels CD
CD player
one Talking Stick and one Listening Stick—wooden dowels or branches, about 12 to 18 inches long, decorated with paints, markers, cloth, yarn, feathers, jewelry, or carved designs

Directions

1. Listen to the song "That's What I Like about You" with a group of eight to ten children.
2. Ask the children to remember some of the positive statements in the song.
3. Show the Talking and Listening Sticks to the group. Explain that only the person holding the Talking Stick will be allowed to speak.
4. Choose one child from the group to hold the Talking and Listening Sticks.
5. Have the child give the Listening Stick to another child.
6. Ask the child with the Talking Stick to say one positive thing about the child with the Listening Stick.
7. The child with the Listening Stick then takes the Talking Stick and gives the Listening Stick to another child. The process is repeated with the next child.

Discussion

If the children are having a hard time thinking of things to say, ask the whole group some of these questions:

- What is something that this person seems to enjoy doing? What are they good at?
- When is this person helpful?
- Has this person done something that made you happy?

Additional question for older children that will help them think about the skills involved in talking and listening:

- Which do you like best—talking or listening?
- Which did you find the hardest? Why?
- How can you tell when someone is really listening to you?

Variations

1. If you are concerned that one or more children in the group will be left out, you can change the structure of the activity. In a group of four to eight children, give each child a turn to hold the Listening Stick. On each child's turn, pass the Talking Stick around the circle. After everyone says something positive about the child with the Listening Stick, pass the Listening Stick to the next person. Repeat.

2. The Talking Stick can also be used to facilitate group discussions by helping children pay attention to one speaker at a time. Talking and Listening Sticks are also useful in conflict resolution.

3. The children can make their own Talking and Listening Sticks, or a group of children can work together to design a set. Or use special rocks or flags. For children who are unable to hold an object, try using hats or blankets.

4. Find or make a special bag or box to hold your class Listening and Talking Sticks.

Ages: 4–8

LETTERS TO MYSELF

Here is an activity that gives a child the chance to say something positive about a very important person.

Materials

paper
marking pens, crayons, or pencils
envelopes

Directions

1. Ask the children to think about something they like about themselves. You may want to give them a sentence to complete, such as, "I like me when I . . ." Have the children write down their ideas, or have an adult write them down.

2. Ask the children to draw pictures to illustrate their statements.

3. Give the children envelopes. Help them fold their pictures and enclose them in the envelopes.

4. Help the children put their names on the envelopes. Older children can print their names and addresses. Send the envelopes home, either with the children or in the mail.

Discussion

Use these questions to help the children think about themselves:

- What do you like to do that is fun?
- What do you like to learn about? What is something you learned in the last few days?
- What is your favorite time of the day? Why?
- What are some things that you can do really well?

Variations

1. Have the children trace their own or each others' handprints and write their letter around it.

2. Create a display of the children's letters, then send them home after a few days.

3. Ask the children to write letters on what they like about their families.

4. For the visually impaired, or for those who are unable to draw, use a tape recorder and let the child describe what they like about themselves.

5. In some families and cultures, "bragging" about oneself is discouraged. If you know that your classroom includes people from these backgrounds, change the activity for the whole class so that it focuses on others. Children can write letters to their friends, neighbors, or relatives.

Ages: 3–8

For young children, school is often the first community institution where they spend time away from their families. When children feel good about their school and community, they feel better about themselves. Does your school provide children with a positive model of what a community can be?

Materials

one or more cameras with enough film that each child can take at least three pictures (one-use cameras will work well)
clipboard, pen, and paper
index cards

Directions

1. Ask the children in your class to think about what they like about their school. Let them know that each child will be able to take three pictures of their favorite people or places in the school.

2. In small groups of up to four children, walk around your school, inside and out. Ask the children to tell you what they would like to photograph. Many children will want to take all of their pictures immediately; you can help these children be more thoughtful about their choices by touring your school first and writing down each child's choices, then returning to take the photos. Let each child take up to three pictures (the youngest children or children with limited arm strength may need an adult to take the photo; older children will be able to do it themselves). Use the clipboard to make notes about which picture each child takes.

3. Create a display in your room called What I Like about My School. As you get your photos printed, let each child choose one of their photos for the display. Ask the children to describe their photos, telling you what they like about the parts of the school they chose. Write their comments down on the index cards and add them to the display.

Discussion

You can help the children decide what they want to photograph by asking them these questions as you look around your school:

- Where are your favorite places at our school? What are your favorite things to do?
- Where at our school do you like to play and learn?
- Which places do you think are beautiful?
- Who are your favorite people here at school?

Variations

1. As the children get older, they are able to think about the wider neighborhood around their school. Have the children choose sites that they like in the neighborhood and make a What I Like about Our Neighborhood display.

Ages: 3–8

INVOLVING FAMILIES: FAMILY DISPLAYS

To help children be proud of themselves, we need to help them feel proud of their families. This activity gives every family a chance to share interests and materials that are important to them.

Materials

table, shelf, or other display space in the classroom
materials for display background, such as cloth and papers

Directions

1. Send a letter to the families describing the Family Displays project (see sample letter).
2. You may have a staff member set up the first display about their own family, to give everyone an idea of the project.
3. Post a sign-up sheet and calendar where the families can choose a time slot.
4. A few days before a family's time slot, remind them to bring in their materials.
5. When a family brings in their display material, let them arrange it however they want. Help them make labels and signs that are appropriate for the age of the children in your classroom. Some families may want to write or dictate stories.
6. At group time, ask the child if he or she would like to tell the group about the items on display or if you can read the family's words.
7. Ask if anyone has questions. If the child can't answer the questions, write them down and ask the family.

Discussion

After the children have had the chance to see a variety of family displays, you can use them to bring out the similarities and differences among families by asking questions, such as:

- Do you remember items from the family displays that were similar to each other? How were they the same?
- Was there an item you remember that was unique, unlike any other?

- Was there an item from another family's display that reminded you of your own family?
- What items can you remember that were used for eating? For wearing? For working? For celebrating?

Variations

1. Ask the families to bring in something from their child's infancy—baby clothes, pictures, toys, birth announcements, and so on. Set up a display that includes several families at one time.
2. Ask the families to bring an item from home that is a particular color. Create a display based on that color.

A sample letter for the Family Displays project:

Dear Families,

We are talking about families in our classroom, including all the ways families are the same and the ways they are different. We want every child to feel proud of their family and to accept that others can be proud of their family, as well, even if they are different.

We would like to invite you to bring in a picture of your family and some things that you feel represent it and your child. These could be activities you like to do together, items that you use for holidays or rituals, things you have made, or items that reflect your heritage.

We are creating a special place in the room where we can help each family set up their display for a week at a time. While we will do our best to keep your materials safe, we don't recommend bringing items that are irreplaceable or fragile.

Our first display will be about our head teacher and her family. Be sure to check it out, and let us know when you will be able to participate.

Thanks for being your child's best teacher—

The Power in Me

11

POWER!

It's a subject preschoolers find fascinating. And why not? As toddlers, they learned to walk and talk. They took charge of feeding themselves and mastered the potty. They feel grown-up, in control, and ready to conquer the world.

Except the world turns out to be a lot bigger than they imagined. As they venture into school and the neighborhood, they discover that their home and family aren't necessarily the center of the universe and that they are not quite as big and strong as they want to be. Is it any wonder that so many preschoolers long for superpowers and want to use our culture's most prominent symbol of power—a gun?

Play is one way that young children investigate big questions. By taking their ideas and turning them into action—into things they can touch, see, and talk about—they are better able to understand how the world works. "How can I feel powerful?" is one of these big questions, and children of this age want tangible power symbols to hold and wear while they explore it. We can help them create materials that focus their play on helping others, rather than the negative vision of aggression and weaponry they pick up from the media.

But even as they play out their wishes, they need to be reminded that their real power lies inside of them, just like it did when they took their first steps or said their first words. "The Power in Me" can show them that, in the long run, their intelligence, imagination, and compassion will provide the power that they seek, and that helping others is the best way to feel good about yourself. The activities that accompany the song are designed to help children understand and use power in a positive way, both in their play and in the bigger world.

Here are some children's books that you can use when discussing all the ways people can use their power:

Baker, Keith. *The Magic Fan.* San Diego: Harcourt Brace, 1989.

Brown, Laurie K. *Dinosaurs to the Rescue!* Boston: Little, Brown and Company, 1994

Fassler, Joan. *Howie Helps Himself.* Morton Grove, Illinois: Albert Whitman, 1987.

Hoffman, Eric. *Heroines and Heroes.* St. Paul: Redleaf Press, 1999.

Perry, Sarah. *If . . .* New York: Oxford University Press, 1995.

Ringgold, Faith. *Tar Beach.* New York: Crown, 1991.

THE POWER IN ME

Sometimes in my dreams I fly,_____ And magic powers help me, I've saved cities, I've saved lives, Just like I've seen on TV,_____ But when my dreams are resting, And my day is going to start, I know I'll still have mighty power All inside my heart._____

Everyone has the strength inside, No need to push_ and shove, Everyone can be a hero Using the power of their love. It's not a magic laser beam, A play gun or a sword, I use the power in my heart, It's stronger than a toy._____

©1996
Words by Cathy Fink (2 Spoons Music, ASCAP)
Music by Ken Whitely (Pair A Dice Music, SOCAN)

The Power in Me

by Cathy Fink (lyrics) and Ken Whitely (music)
(©1996 Cathy Fink and Ken Whitely)

Sometimes in my dreams I fly,
And magic powers help me,
I've saved cities, I've saved lives,
Just like I've seen on TV,
But when my dreams are resting,
And my day is going to start,
I know I'll still have mighty power
All inside my heart.

Everyone has the strength inside,
No need to push and shove,
Everyone can be a hero
Using the power of their love.
It's not a magic laser beam,
A play gun or a sword,
I use the power in my heart,
It's stronger than a toy.

chorus:
The power is in my heart,
It comes from deep inside,
Where I love from, where I start,
Where I laugh, and where I cry.
Every boy and girl
Has power just like me
Use my feelings, use my words,
Right next door, around the world.
Be as powerful as I can be,
I'm gonna be as powerful as I can be.

Inside me I find
The courage that I need
To try to do something new
And even ask for help from you
The power in me helps me to grow
Every single day
Learn to share, learn to care
In my work and play

chorus

I've got the power to think. Oh, yes!
I've got the power to learn. Oh, yes!
I've got the power to love. Oh, yes!
I've got the power to dream. Oh, yes!
I've got the power to grow. Oh, yes!
I've got the power to speak. Oh, yes!
I've got the power to play. Oh, yes!
I've got the power to share. Oh, yes!

THE HEROINES AND HEROES CAVE

Young children want to carry on their quest for power in their play. Instead of relying on TV shows that accentuate the violent use of power, set up a fantasy play area that allows the children to practice pro-social skills. Listening to the song "The Power in Me" provides an inspirational introduction to this activity.

Materials

Changing Channels CD

CD player

materials to create a cave, such as blankets, tarps, a large box, a tent, or an empty cabinet

materials to make "rock" decorations for the cave, such as brown or gray construction paper

paper or cloth, scissors, and glitter paints

materials to make "medals," such as ribbon or yarn and cardboard circles or juice can lids

power paraphernalia, such as fancy bracelets, headbands, capes, and hats

Directions

1. At group time, play the song "The Power in Me."

2. Ask the children if they have ever dreamed of being heroines or heroes who help someone. Have them tell you some of the stories they have imagined.

3. Introduce the idea of a Heroines and Heroes Cave. Tell the children you want to make a special place where they can create and play out more stories about helping and rescuing people. Make up a story with the children. You may need to provide the first lines of the story (see sample below).

4. Build a Heroines and Heroes Cave, indoors or out, large enough to hold at least four children. Attach blankets or tarps to fences, tables, or climbing structures, cut openings in a large appliance box, cover the inside of a cabinet with cloth, or set up a tent—create an interesting space! Older children can help design and build it.

5. Set up a shelf or table nearby for the power paraphernalia.

6. Set up a table with art materials for making "rocks." Ask the children to cut out rock shapes from the papers—younger children may need some assistance. Let them decorate the rock shapes with glitter glue or other fancy decorations.

7. When the projects are dry, let the children decorate the cave with them. Keep some materials available at all times so the children can continue decorating.

8. Make medals using cardboard shapes, glitter paint, and yarn or ribbon, or with juice can lids that have a hole punched in them (take care to knock off any sharp points).

9. Make up more rescue stories at group times with the whole class and throughout the day with smaller groups interested in the area. Write down some of their stories. Give medals to all who participate.

10. Add props to the area as needed. For example, you may add stuffed animals to be rescued, lengths of fancy ribbon or yarn for rescue ropes, gold-painted rocks, small ladders, and rescue vehicles.

Discussion

Help the children create their stories by asking them these questions when they can't come up with ideas:

- Who will need help in your story? Why do they need help?
- How do you know that they want you to help them?
- How can you help them?
- What are the kinds of powers that are mentioned in the song "The Power in Me"? How can you use them in your story?
- What are some of the powerful things you can do together with friends to help people in your story?

Variations

1. Make a large Heroines and Heroes Cave flag or banner as an art project. Use cloth and watercolors or markers.

2. Add a table-size Heroines and Heroes Cave to your block area to use with small dolls.

3. Keep a tape recorder inside the cave for the children to dictate stories.

Variations continue on next page

4. Alternatives to caves include castles, forts, boats, and airplanes. Follow the interests of the children!

5. Can a wheelchair get into your Heroines and Heroes Cave? If not, let your young heroines and heroes figure out how to make it accessible as a real-life project. What can they use to add a ramp or enlarge the entranceway? If you have a person who uses a wheelchair in your school community, ask if they would consult with the children and help them test their ideas. Otherwise, try to borrow a wheelchair from a local medical office.

A sample Heroines and Heroes Cave rescue story, created with four preschoolers:

Teacher: Amos, Luciana, Sheila, and Marcus were crawling into the Heroines and Heroes Cave when they heard someone calling, "Help! Meow! Help!" What do you think happened?

Children: They ran out to find it and help it. It was a cat. There was a lake, as big as the whole school. A boat was in the lake, but it was tipped over; the cat was falling out. She was fishing and the fish pulled her over, and cats hate water! She was so scared! We all got in our superpower boats and raced to her and threw a golden rope into the water, but it was too slippery. Oh, no! Poor kitty! She was saying, "Meow! Meow! Help me!" We threw her a ladder, but it was too heavy and it sank to the bottom. So we all jumped in the water and swam with our capes on, and we held hands. The kitty jumped onto our capes and held on with her claws but she didn't hurt us. Then we swam back to the beach. Everyone was breathing, and we got hot and dried off. The cat said, "I am the queen's cat and you have saved me. She will give you lots of gold, and she will give you medals, because you are the bravest in the world, and everyone will shout hooray!" So they went to the castle and had a big party. Hooray!

POWER TOOL BOXES

Fantasy rescue stories are a fun way for children to envision what they can do in the future, but there are ways children can help each other right now—using Power Tools. Here are ideas for three different Power Tool Boxes; make up your own for any helping job that comes up regularly in your classroom.

Materials

lunchboxes or other containers of similar size, one for each Power Tool Box you want to make

Medical Tool Box: several bandages, a packet of moist towelettes, a packet of tissues, small-size disposable gloves, a plastic bag, stethoscope, and materials for a "rice baby" (an old sock and rice)

Spill Cleanup Tool Box: a small towel, sponge, small sweep brush and dustpan, and a plastic bag

Book Repair Tool Box: scissors and two rolls of clear book-repair tape, one narrow and one wide

Directions

1. If the lunchboxes or containers you choose have commercial logos on them, cover with white construction paper or Con-Tact paper. Label and decorate each with appropriate words, pictures, or drawings. The children can help decorate the boxes.

2. Add to the box whatever tools the children would need to help out in the classroom. For example, the medical kit should have supplies that children can use to help each other with minor injuries. (Injuries that might lead to contact with another person's blood or other body fluids should always be handled by an adult.) The children can make "rice babies" by filling clean, old socks with rice and tying a knot at the end. These can be kept in the freezer for bumps and bruises.

3. Create a Power Tools place on a shelf that the children can reach. Let the children know that the Tool Boxes are only to be used when someone really needs help.

4. When you need help with a task, ask a child to get the proper Power Tool Box. For example, when a child falls and scrapes a knee, and you determine that the injury can be handled by other children, choose someone to get the Medical Tool Box. (If one child has hurt another, the child who did the hurting is often the

best one to get the box.) Add a rice baby to the box if it seems to be needed. Ask the children which tools they think will be the most helpful to use, and supervise their safe use. Even though the stethoscope isn't a necessity, the children will always choose it!

5. When you are done using a Power Tool Box, ask the children what they think the box needs so that it can be ready to use again. Help the children clean up or replace whatever needs renewing, and put the box back in its place.

Discussion

Here are some questions you can ask when you introduce and use the Power Tool Boxes:

- Adults who help others often carry tools. What kinds of tools would a grown-up use in a medical emergency? To help clean up a big mess? To help repair furniture or other equipment?
- Before you help others with the Power Tools, you have to find out if they want to be helped. How can you find this out?
- Some Power Tools need to get their power from electricity. Where does the power for these tools come from?
- Some TV shows, movies, and books have characters with super-powers. What makes something a superpower? Do people really have superpowers? Do you need superpowers to help people?

Variation

1. If a Tool Box is very popular, you may want to make several of the same kind.

2. Add a hat, armband, or necklace to each box for a child to wear while using the tools. For example, a Medical Tool Box could have several armbands with red crosses.

3. Instead of boxes, use tool belts that you can hang up: fanny packs, carpenter's bags, or a belt with pockets made out of the ends of socks.

4. For children who do not have the physical dexterity to open boxes, attach each tool to a board with a Velcro fastener. Try to get tools that can be used by those children, or attach tools to gloves, straps, or handles to make them easier to manipulate. Even if the child is not able to use a tool, he or she will be able to participate by handing tools to an adult or another child as they are needed.

5. Give medals to everyone involved!

Ages: 5–8

Wishes and Dreams Time Capsule

Allowing children to use their power to dream and to envision a hopeful future is essential if we want them to use their powers to help create a better world. A Wishes and Dreams Time Capsule can help children become aware of their own powerful dreams.

Materials

paper
markers, crayons, or colored pencils
cardboard box or other container, about 1 by 1 by 1 foot

Directions

1. Near the beginning of the school year, ask the children, "Do you have any powerful wishes or dreams for yourself?" Ask the children who respond if they would like to draw a picture of their wish or have you write down their words. Let the children know that you will be putting their responses in a Wishes and Dreams Time Capsule. You may have to explain that a time capsule is a box that you put things in and hide away, then open up after some time has passed so you can remember what happened. Some time capsules contain photographs, inventions, or newspapers, but your time capsule will hold several kinds of wishes and dreams. It will take all week to make.

2. Have the children place their pictures or stories in the box.

3. On the second day, ask the children to think of a powerful wish or dream they have for their family. Add these to the time capsule.

4. On the third day, ask the children if they have any powerful wishes or dreams for their friends to add to the time capsule.

5. On the fifth day, ask if they have any wishes for the whole world.

6. When you have gathered all the pictures and stories in the box, tape or glue it shut. The children may want to help you decorate the time capsule. Use markers or crayons, or glue on fancy papers, jewels, feathers, glitter, and so on. Label the box Wishes and Dreams Time Capsule.

7. Decide with the class where you should keep the time capsule. Let them know that you will be opening it in about four months.

8. In the middle of the year, open the time capsule to see if any of the wishes and dreams came true. Let the children make new wishes. Reseal the box.

9. Open the time capsule again at the end of the school year or at an end-of-the-year celebration.

Discussion

Here are some questions to help the children think about wishes and dreams:

- What do you want to learn this year? Is there something new you want to try?
- Do you want to do something special this year?
- Can you think of someone you could help? How?

These questions will help older children think about what wishes and dreams are:

- What is the difference between a dream you have in your sleep and a dream that you wish for when you are awake?
- Some wishes might come true some day. Are there any of your wishes that are impossible and could never come true? Why?

Variations

1. Add a class picture to your time capsule so the children can see how much they have grown.

2. Some children, particularly those with limited vision, will want to use a tape recorder to record their wishes.

3. Older children can make a time capsule by covering a balloon with papier-mâché. Break open your time capsule piñata-style. Before you close up the time capsule, add some small treats. When it's time to open the capsule, hang it up, and give everyone two or three chances to break it with a broom handle or bat. Older children can do this blindfolded. When the capsule breaks, everyone can grab a treat and pick one picture or story to take to the person who created it.

Involving Families: Power Helper Coupon Booklets

Adults often focus on the times children are not successful and forget to notice children when they are using their power wisely. Here's a simple, concrete way to help families pay attention to those times.

Materials

copies of the Power Helper Coupon (see sample below)
stapler
instruction letter (see below)

Directions

1. Make Power Helper Coupon Booklets by stapling together six to ten copies of the Power Helper Coupons. You may want to add a colored cover.

2. Give a coupon booklet and instruction letter to every family.

3. Over the next week, ask the families if they have used the coupons and how they have used them. Once you have heard that several families have given them out, ask the children at group time if anyone has received any Power Helper Coupons. Let each child tell the story of how they earned their coupons.

4. When the families use up their coupons, give them more.

Discussion

You can help support family participation in this activity by asking the children these questions at school:

- How do you use your power to help people at school? Can you do the same kind of job at home?
- How do people help you? Can you help other people in the same way?

Variations

1. Ask families to write down or dictate some of the ways their children have earned coupons. Create a Power Helper Story Book with the descriptions.

2. If there are families who don't participate, give out coupons at school, especially to those children who don't have the opportunity to earn them at home.

3. Once you have heard that everyone in the class has earned at least one coupon, plan a Power Helper Celebration and invite families to attend. This could be a tea party, an award ceremony, a ritual, a potluck meal, and/or a sing-along. Each family can share one story and everyone can get medals.

A Power Helper Coupon Booklet Sample Letter:

Dear Families,

Young children often feel very small, and surrounded by a very big world. They want to feel powerful, but don't always know how to do it. Some children get the idea from TV and movies that the way to be powerful is to fight. We want the children in our classroom to discover that they feel strong when they use their power to help others. We would like you to help your child learn this important lesson.

A Power Helper Coupon Booklet is attached to this letter. When your child uses the power of his or her body, mind, or heart to help someone, fill out a coupon and give it to your child. While we don't recommend that you give rewards along with it, such as candy or special privileges, we do encourage you to give your child plenty of thanks and hugs.

You may want to create a place to display the coupons your child has earned. How about on your refrigerator door? If others in your family want to participate, give them coupons too—we have plenty of booklets that you can take home.

Let us know when you have given coupons to your child. We will be setting up other activities at school to go along with this program—we'll let you know in the next few weeks what we have planned.

Thanks for being your child's best teacher—

Other Resources from Redleaf Press

Help Yourself! Activities to Promote Safety and Self-Esteem
by Kate Ross
Contains fun and creative ways to use the songs from the CD *Help Yourself* as a springboard into a curriculum for promoting self-esteem and safety skills among young children.

Before Push Comes to Shove: Building Conflict Resolution Skills with Children
by Nancy Carlsson-Paige & Diane E. Levin
A curriculum guide for helping adults teach conflict-resolution skills to children. Suggested for use with the children's book *Best Day of the Week*.

Best Day of the Week
by Nancy Carlsson-Paige
The story of Angela and Calvin and how they resolve their play-related differences constructively.

The Kindness Curriculum: Introducing Young Children to Loving Values
by Judith Anne Rice
Create opportunities for children to practice kindness, empathy, conflict resolution, and respect.

Making it Better: Activities for Children Living in a Stressful World
by Barbara Oehlberg
This important book offers bold new information about the physical and emotional effects of stress, trauma, and violence on children today, and gives teachers and caregivers the confidence to help children survive, thrive, and learn.

The Optimistic Classroom: Creative Ways to Give Children Hope
by Deborah Hewitt and Sandra Heidemann
Over seventy activities will develop ten strengths that allow children to meet and cope with the challenges they face.

What the Kids Said Today: Using Classroom Conversations to Become a Better Teacher
by Daniel Gartrell
Contains 145 stories that explore how teachers can use conversations with children to build skills such as acceptance, cooperation, creative and peaceful problem solving, and appropriate emotional expression.

Practical Solutions to Practically Every Problem: The Early Childhood Teacher's Manual
by Steffen Saifer
Over 300 proven, developmentally appropriate solutions for all kinds of classroom problems.

800-423-8309
www.redleafpress.org

4577